Nobodies to Somebodies

Nobodies to Somebodies

*A Practical Theology for
Education and Liberation*

Anthony G. Reddie

To Ira. Williams
7 Sefton Park Rd
Br

EPWORTH PRESS

British Library Cataloguing in Publication data

A catalogue record for this book is available
from the British Library

0 7162 0558 0

First published in 2003
by Epworth Press
4 John Wesley Road
Werrington
Peterborough, PE4 7ZP

Typeset by Regent Typesetting, London
Printed and bound in Great Britain
by Biddles Ltd, www.biddles.co.uk

Contents

Dedication

To my family
In every part of the world
And for those
In the next world
And in the
World to come

Without you
I would not be.

Acknowledgements

I have spent all my life in the church. When I saw an advert for a
Christian education worker to undertake research on behalf of the
Birmingham District of the Methodist Church (in conjunction with
the Connexional/National Church), looking at the Christian education and nurture of Black youth in inner-city churches, I jumped at
the chance. This was my opportunity to seek answers to a number of
longstanding questions that had been floating around in my mind
for many years. The work of this project, which forms the major
part of this book, was called the Birmingham Initiative.

When I began working on this project, I set myself a number of
quite exacting targets. The final target was to complete a major
piece of work that would document the important themes and issues
that arose from this research project. In the first instance this work
owes its existence to the foresight of the Revd Christopher Hughes
Smith.[1] Chris remains a staunch supporter of this work. I am also
grateful to the whole of Methodism for its continued support.
Despite occasional outbursts of frustrated passion and dissatisfaction, Methodism remains my spiritual home and I am wedded to it
by bonds that have lasted a lifetime. Special thanks are reserved for
the Pastoral Care and Christian Education Office of the Connexional team, plus the Formation in Ministry and the Racial
Justice offices for their particular support.

Additional thanks are due to the Queens Foundation, in
Birmingham. The space afforded me in the Research Centre has
been priceless in enabling this work to be completed so quickly.

When I commenced the research that would culminate in this
book, one of the first significant meetings I attended was the monthly Black Theology in Britain forum in Selly Oak, Birmingham.

Given the challenges of being a Black Christian educator and scholar in a wholly White discipline in Britain, I remain grateful to this interdisciplinary forum for providing me with an intellectual home from where I could spread my academic wings.

Extended thanks are offered to the many children, young people, adult lay leaders and ministers who have contributed to this work. You have all been truly gracious and I am profoundly grateful. Thanks are extended to the Revd Dr Emmanuel Jacob, whose assistance in shaping the book has been invaluable.

Finally, my heartfelt thanks are for the wonderful people at Moseley Road Methodist Church in Balsall Heath, Birmingham. The members of this church have become like a second family to me over the years. It is a place which, despite its perennial struggles and difficulties, has a certain magic to it that I have yet to experience in any other church. For all the people at Moseley Road and those further afield whose experiences are reflected in this work, I hope you feel it has done you justice.

Introduction

Chapter 1 is entitled 'Who Feels It, Knows It'. This chapter commences with an outline of the context of the work, along with a brief section on how the study was conducted, which is followed in turn by some opening theological reflections on the theme of *Nobodies to Somebodies*. The sociocultural, theological and educational background follows these opening sections. In it I offer a rationale for this work, detailing my commitment to this particular inquiry and the necessity for the creation and development of the approach to Christian education recommended in the book.

While every attempt has been made to ensure that this book is accessible to many people, particularly those who are not academics, it should be noted that this first chapter requires more effort to follow than the subsequent sections of the book. This is due to the need to introduce readers to a number of important theories and ideas that underpin this work. I hope you will feel able to stay with it, as the concerns outlined in this chapter will become more apparent and clear when you read the later sections of the book.

In Chapter 2, 'Pioneers Along the Way', I outline the case for an African-centred approach to Christian education. This chapter begins with a historical overview, highlighting the important studies that investigated the different approaches to the task of teaching the Christian faith to people of African descent. This section analyses the theological and educational imperatives for this approach to Christian education, and in particular, the influence of Black and liberation theologies. Having analysed previous efforts at constructing appropriate pedagogies (or strategies for teaching) for Black people, the chapter concludes by outlining the central task of attempting to create an appropriate model for the British context.

In Chapter 3, entitled 'Bringing the Thing to Life', I begin the task of highlighting the theological and educational tools I employed in order to create a new model of Christian education for Britain. In this section of the book I outline the content and educational philosophy of this new model or programme. The latter part of the chapter looks at the disparities in theory and practice of Christian education. I investigate the educational and practical challenges of creating a suitable curriculum. The final part of the chapter outlines the attempts at piloting the work. The primary question is posed: What emerged through this relationship between theory and practice? The answers to this question are, in part, exemplified in the creation of *Growing into Hope*, the two-volume curriculum that emerged from this study. This chapter and the following sections of the book analyse the creation of these land-mark publications – the first examples of a systematic Black, African-centred Christian education programme in Britain.

Chapter 4, entitled 'Making it Work', details the process of piloting this new model. Using a number of case studies, I demonstrate how, through the piloting of this programme, a number of inner-city churches (predominantly Methodist, plus Anglican and Baptist) were able to bring to life many of the substantive elements of Black theology, and so begin to change their practice. This newly developed model of Christian education reflects the culture of Black experience, expression, history and identity, while also being open and accessible to many people, in terms of ethnicity, gender and age. These case study accounts are supplemented by further investigation into the literature (once again, attempting to create a continuing relationship between theory and practice), plus a number of interviews with Black children and young people, who played a pivotal role in the study.

In Chapter 5, entitled 'The Way it Should Be?', I seek to describe and analyse various attempts to consolidate and affirm this new model of Christian teaching and learning. In this section I describe the contextual and historical difficulties associated with the creation of a new basis on which Black culture, experience and expression can be affirmed and legitimated within churches where Eurocentric norms have predominated.

I

'Who Feels It, Knows It': Socio-political and Cultural Background

Setting the context

This book is concerned with the task of creating a new model or example of Christian education, which is informed by and reflects the needs of Black children and young people[1] living in Britain. This new model is a particular understanding of the relationship between theology and education. The two major areas that contribute to this work are the disciplines of Black and Womanist theology[2] and transformative education. (The nature and importance of these disciplines will be highlighted in Chapter 2). While the subject of this book is concerned with the task of creating a practical, liberating model of Black Christian education for the British context, this work falls into the wider, more global title of *practical theology*.

Black Christian education as a form of practical theology

Practical theology can be understood in a number of ways.[3] This particular version of theology is based on the process of teaching and learning. Practical theology is essentially a continuing dialogue between the many ways in which people think about God, and how these ideas and forms of understanding are practised, i.e., it is a dialogue between theory and practice. A natural feature of this approach to the relationship between the theory and practice of theology (i.e., 'practical theology') is the presence of what is often termed 'theological reflection'. In using this term we are talking of the ways in which ideas about God are investigated (the term 'interrogate' is often used) in the hope that what emerges from this process is a model of learning that will be liberating for Black people.

It is my belief that Black Christian education is a branch of practical theology and, as such, has an important part to play in the world of academic theology. With its emphasis upon the practical task of teaching and learning the Christian faith, Black Christian education has, as its central concern, the desire that the gospel of Jesus Christ should liberate and transform Black people. This aspect should be discerned within the educational processes that are arranged in order that the learner should learn more about God. This task is theological, for it is concerned with seeking to understand more about God, the Scriptures and the ongoing relationship between God and humankind. It is a form of practical theology, for it seeks to create a form of progression by which the Christian faith can be declared and lived out with integrity and assurance.[4] While there is much within the discipline of Christian education that can be abstract or difficult, the ultimate aim, however, is the creation of learning opportunities for Christian believers or those who have not been exposed to the gospel of Christ. In this respect, it is intensely theological and essentially practical.

It could be argued that the development of Black theology in Britain[5] despite its growing strength and influence has, like its more established transatlantic cousin in the USA, yet to develop a form of practical action to match the potency of its ideas. In creating a Black Christian education of liberation, this work is both an educational and a theological text. It is a practical theology of liberation for all people within the British context.

Central to the task of creating a new model for the Christian education and nurture of Black youth has been the development of an African–centred Christian education curriculum. This programme combines the insights of Black and womanist theology and transformative education in order to create the first Black Christian education of liberation for this country. Through the development of this programme and additional materials, I have attempted to change and improve the practice of the teaching and learning of the Christian faith for children of African descent.

Definition of key terms

Before we get into the heart of this work, I believe it is important to clarify a number of potential queries or concerns. In the first instance, it should be noted that throughout the book the terms 'African-Caribbean' and 'Black' are used. While I am aware that there are important differences between these two terms, I have sought to use both categories to highlight the specific and the shared concerns of people of African descent. The term 'African-Caribbean' is used in a very specific sense to refer to children and young people whose immediate parentage or more immediate forebears are from the Caribbean. This term is not intended to be exclusive, i.e., it does not relegate or ignore the claims and presence of those people who might describe themselves as being *African*. The term 'African' refers to individuals and groups whose parentage and immediate forebears are from the African continent. I use it to highlight the experiences of the group of people with whom this research was conducted. The majority of Black people, in historic-mainline churches in Birmingham, would be described as being African-Caribbean.

When I use the term 'African-Caribbean', particularly within the context of my research in Birmingham, I am mindful of the fact that a significant proportion of members of inner-city churches in London, for example, are *African*. This work is as much about the experiences of this latter group as it is of those who might describe themselves as being African-Caribbean.

In a White majority country, such as Britain, there is a unified, common experience of struggle and marginalization, which transcends particular issues of regionalism or the oceanic divide between Africa and the Caribbean. The term 'Black' unites all peoples of African descent in solidarity with all oppressed peoples of the world. The example of Christian education commended in this book is a model of teaching and learning for every Black majority church in Britain and beyond – a model that acknowledges its own particularity, but which attempts to speak to the different traditions, denominations and theological perspectives that exist here.

This book details the groundbreaking activity of the Birmingham Initiative – a project that took the collective and individual stories of Black people seriously, in order to use these resources as the primary tools for undertaking theological reflection. It is the story of how a number of Black people in a group of inner-city churches took the momentous journey from being *Nobodies to Somebodies*.

How the work was undertaken

This study was undertaken with faith communities within the historic-mainline tradition.[6] In terms of the method of the research, I decided to work as a subjective insider – as someone who is within the environment in which the research is taking place and is, therefore, affected by what happens within that specific setting. I wanted to align myself with African-Caribbean children in the various cultural arenas where Christian education was undertaken. I was nurtured and educated into the Christian faith from within the Methodist tradition. In order to act as a subjective insider I wanted to concentrate my efforts upon cultural and religious settings that were familiar to me.

I decided to locate my activities within those churches that are synonymous with European traditions and cultures – those churches that came into contact with African people during the era of slavery. The exporting of such denominations as Anglicanism, Methodism, Presbyterianism and the Baptist traditions to the Caribbean led to a cultural discord between White European norms and the belief systems of Black slaves that were carried over from the continent of Africa.[7] The development of this new model for a Black Christian education of liberation was accomplished through the piloting of experimental teaching and learning schemes in these churches.

In choosing to confine my study largely to historic-mainline churches, I wanted to investigate the religious and cultural environment of these varied settings. Beckford has called these institutions the 'slave master's house'.[8] I wanted to see whether the extremes of worshipping within a White institution and the developing liberation movements in these settings might offer tentative models for critical change in other, less entrenched and difficult environments. My understanding of the process of liberation is that it invariably emerges from the margins. In the context of Black expression and identity I would argue that the extremes of this critical struggle are to be found in the inhibited and repressed thinking and emotions of Black people within historic-mainline traditions. In seeking to liberate Black people in one particular context, it may well be the case that this research might offer insights for African and African-Caribbean peoples in other repressive religious and cultural situations.

Opening reflections: nobodies to somebodies

The following reflections are based upon the sketched outline of three figures in silhouette at the front of this book. This image also adorns the front covers of *Growing into Hope*, the two volumes of Christian education materials that arose out of the study and which also serve as the basis of this book. I would invite you to look again at that image of the three figures. Hold those figures in your mind as you consider the following reflections.

When I began undertaking this work back in 1995, I was confronted, at that time, by a seemingly all pervasive conspiracy of silence. Having been nurtured and socialized within the Methodist Church, I had seen the extent to which the perspectives of Black people and their concerns and experiences were often trivialized and disregarded.

In the course of doing this work, I have been strengthened and affirmed by the Black Theology in Britain support group, which meets in Selly Oak, Birmingham on a monthly basis. On the occasions when I have spoken about my work in the area of Christian education, I have had cause to lament the seemingly pervasive conspiracy of silence in which I am operating.

For while the group as a whole is committed to the shared task of pursuing Black theological conversation and study, I am struck continuously by the dearth of Black Christian educators. There exists in Britain a growing number of Black theologians, particularly in the area of systematics and pastoral care. Certainly, I would agree that there are not enough in our number, but our company is being swelled by new members all the time. Less apparent is the growth in academic Black Christian educators. This lack, in some respects, reflects the weak state of Christian education in Britain as a whole. The number of scholars in this area is not huge. In the area of practice, budgets are being cut, professional staff are being made redundant and, within the church, resources (both financial and human) are seemingly non-existent.

If the state of Christian education is in need of resuscitation, then the plight of Christian education, as it applies to Black people, is even worse. While all the aforementioned apply in the area of Black Christian education, this area is marginalized to an even greater extent as a result of the conspiracy of silence. In institutional terms, Christian education in Britain has been the whitest, and most middle-class of all enterprises. If you were to look in the shelves of the most reputable Christian bookshops, particularly in the area of Christian education, nurture, worship and learning, you would be hard pressed to find a non-White face. The writers, the various materials, the stories of faith, the prayers, liturgies, etc. are virtually all White. The publication of *Tuesday's Child*,[9] a potted historical survey of the development of Christian education covering the twentieth century, only serves to amplify my point. In what is otherwise a very impressive publication, there is no mention of any development of Christian education that is outside a White Euro-American framework, save for the work of Paulo Freire.

Prior to undertaking this research, I worked as a church-related youth and community worker in Handsworth, Birmingham. The client group, with whom I worked, was mainly African-Caribbean youths. My attempts to find relevant Christian education material that might accord with their experiences bore no fruit.

Upon my appointment to the research post in 1995, I met with many of the 'major' players in Christian education work in England, in order to gain a sense of the current thinking and provisions for work with Black children and young people. In terms of putting names to faces, it was a worthwhile exercise. With reference to the research I was about to undertake, it was futile. Not only was there no work being done in this area, it appeared that there was little appreciation of the differing needs of Black children and young people. There was no attempt to complete the circle of understanding that entails the crossing of cultural boundaries.

Yes, there are increasing numbers of Black majority churches in Britain, particularly in inner-city areas. Yes, it is increasingly the case that a growing number of these churches have youth and children's work that is entirely African and African-Caribbean in complexion. Yes, these churches and the people that attend them are a part of our church, and have been so in large numbers for approaching forty years. But no, we have not done a great deal in terms of trying to address their needs. The teaching and learning of the Christian faith remains academically a White, middle-class affair.

It was into this depressing scene that I took my first tentative steps in the spring of 1995. It appeared that Black young people and children were rendered invisible by the institutional world of Christian education in Britain. With reference to the image at the front of the book (see p. ii), the bottom figure in the crouched position represents, for me, the position of Black people (especially Black children and young people) in terms of our visibility in the religious and wider institutional life of this country. The figure is cowering. We cannot see the face of the figure. This individual has no sense of identity, individuality or visibility.

Theologically, I have likened this bottom figure to that of the woman with the issue of blood in Luke 8.40–48. In the story, we see a woman who is ill physically. She has been unwell for some time and has spent all her savings on trying to become well, or 'whole'. The many doctors she had consulted were unable to make her well. The woman is part of a large crowd. She is not only unwell, she is also anonymous.

I have compared this woman to the situation that confronts many Black children and young people in Britain. (Hereafter, I use the term 'Black youth' or 'young people' to refer to 'children and young people'). The first chapter of this book describes the emotional and psychological pressures that have afflicted Black youth within the larger society and the church over the past fifty years. These struggles and pressures are historic in dimension; their roots lie in the tumult of the slave era, when the African people were demonized and denigrated. The vestiges of that assault upon the African psyche still exist. Black people, particularly young people, can be likened to the woman in the Luke passage. Their malaise may not be a physical one. It is the case, however, that the disproportionately high incidence of mental ill health, poor educational attainment, coupled with institutional pathology and punitive judiciary and criminal systems, have rendered Black youth a problem to be either disregarded or policed in an offensive fashion.

Black youth are at the behest of a state that has rarely taken the time to understand or sought to affirm them. They have been treated as anthropological guinea pigs, to be prodded and poked with derision and suspicion, by the British State, in a manner that accords with the experiences of this woman at the hands of countless doctors. I wonder if she had been viewed as an irritant? Someone to be ignored? Someone to be bullied and controlled? She had no power in her own right.

The power of this story lies in the way in which Jesus acknowledges her presence. She was once anonymous. That is no longer the case. Jesus senses her presence and her needs and plucks her from the crowd. She may well have been startled. Certainly, she would have been very nervous. She may well have been angry with Jesus, initially, for having exposed her to the impatient taunts of the crowd at that particular moment.

By bringing this woman to the central position in this narrative, Jesus breaks her anonymity. The fact that we know of her plight, and are considering its existence in the Luke text, is in itself a testimony to the fact that she will never be forgotten. The woman was already healed *before* Jesus made his announcement, which led to her being exposed. Jesus could have said nothing and let the woman go on her way, healed and untroubled. Jesus, however, does not remain silent. He breaks the silence and creates the opportunity for the woman to move to the centre of the proceedings. She is not only healed, she becomes a 'somebody'.

Returning to the image at the front of the book, I believe that this work is an attempt to turn Black youth (in fact all Black and oppressed peoples) and their accompanying needs and concerns from 'nobodies' to 'somebodies'. The process of change from the figure in the crouched position, to the individual standing tall, proud and visible, is a symbolic representation of the journey from being a 'nobody' to becoming a 'somebody'. This work has been inspired by Jesus' actions in Luke 8 and his engagement with this woman.

While this study has emerged from a very specific location and experience, I believe that the inclusiveness of Black cultures and the expression that arises from it, enables this work to speak to every facet of Christian youth, children's and adult education work in Britain, from whatever cultural background and context that enterprise may emerge. White people are as much in need of liberation as are Black people but, admittedly, for different reasons. We all need the freedom and the confidence to undertake the journey from 'nobodies' to 'somebodies'. This, I believe, has been the prophetic gift of the Birmingham Initiative to the theory and practice of Christian education in Britain.

A short autobiographical sketch

I was born in Bradford, West Yorkshire, of Jamaican parents who arrived in Britain in the late 1950s. Although I was christened in Prospect Hall Methodist Church, my parents changed churches when I was four years old. The church in which I was nurtured and taught the Christian faith was a large city-centre Methodist Mission called Eastbrook Hall. I have often heard people refer to Eastbrook as the Methodist Cathedral of the North. My experiences in this church were largely pleasant and affirming.

While I learnt a great deal on what it was to be a Christian, I learnt nothing about the realities of being a Black person. I do not recall one moment when the culture, traditions and experiences that were so much a part of my home life amongst my family and immediate peers were ever explicitly or implicitly acknowledged within the life of the church. Save for the isolated Sunday reserved for overseas mission, occasions when Black, African-Caribbean life and experiences were expressed and appreciated were conspicuous by their absence. I grew up in an environment where White people and their concerns, cultures and expressions were the norm.

A central feature of my childhood was the imposing picture of Jesus that was situated on the far wall of the room in which the Sunday school met. The Jesus that sat so imposingly on the far wall was a White man, with bright blue eyes and gleaming blond hair. This Jesus, in ethnic terms, was the direct opposite of myself, given my Black skin and African features. The question that arose in my mind was the issue of how could I identify with an incarnate Christ who was so different from me? Within me, there existed a crucial struggle for truth. A struggle with the rhetoric to which I was exposed. One that encouraged me to believe that I was a child of God created in God's image, which sat alongside the reality of this picture that adorned the far wall. Walter Rodney refers to this tension in his analysis of intra-Jamaican sociocultural politics.[10]

This struggle for truth was not resolved during my time in the Sunday school at that church. I was unable to reconcile my Blackness with the overarching depiction of Whiteness within the symbols and language of the Christian faith. This meant that my late teens and early twenties became a time of emotional and psychological struggle.[11] I began to question the desirability of the Christian faith. The image of this White Jesus haunted me. My experiences of alienation from a Eurocentric Christ find accord with the thoughts of Vincent Harding.[12]

It was not until my own investigation into the writings of James Cone and the wider literature of Black and Womanist theology that I began to understand the nature of my Blackness. I saw for the first time the means by which the social, cultural and historical experiences of Black people gave rise to a distinctive expression of Christianity. This distinctive expression was one that was reflected neither within the life of the church nor in the piercing blue eyes of the White Jesus who adorned the wall. It became increasingly clear that if the Christian faith was to become real to me it needed to be appropriated by and approached within an African-centred framework. A framework that both validated and affirmed my identity as a Black person of African descent.

Brief definition of Christian education

The term 'Christian education' can be defined and understood in a variety of ways. Jeff Astley and Colin Crowder provide a helpful starting point for a definition and rationale when they describe it as:

> The phrase . . . often used quite generally to refer to those processes by which people learn to become Christian and to be more Christian, through learning Christian beliefs, attitudes, values, emotions and dispositions to engage in Christian actions and to be open to Christian experiences.[13]

For those wishing to undertake preliminary studies into the theory and practice of Christian education, I would also recommend Jeff Astley's, *The Philosophy of Christian Religious Education*.[14] Chapters 1 and 2 deal with questions of definition, philosophy and the rationale for Christian education.

One must not confuse Christian education, which has a confessional intent to promote Christian belief, with the more professional, sponsored enterprise of religious education that is predominantly associated with county schools. This book is concerned with the former and not the latter.

The development of new approaches and learning materials in Christian education in Britain appears to be general rather than specific. Less emphasis has been placed upon the cultural and ethnic factors that may exist: factors that may have an impact upon the individual's responses to particular educational schemes and the methods employed in their learning and development.

The social, historical and political background

The churches that contributed to this work are all in the inner-city areas of Birmingham. The churches in question have been chosen as those groupings within the historic-mainline tradition that have large numbers of African-Caribbean people within the life of their worshipping community.

The 1945 post-war presence of Black people within inner cities in Britain and the churches to be found there is a hugely significant phenomenon in the recent history of this country. It is often believed that the existence of Black people in Britain can be traced to this period. This influx is perceived as commencing with the arrival of 492 Jamaicans at Tilbury dock on the *Empire Windrush*, 22 June 1948. Yet Ian Duffield quoting from the *Gentlemen's Magazine* of 1764 describes the large numbers of Black people, estimated at the time as high as 20,000, living in London at the turn of the eighteenth century.[15]

Peter Fryer describes the sense of alarm within London society in the later Elizabethan age at the apparent large numbers of Black people (which Fryer estimates to be around 10,000) living in the capital then.[16] Black people lived in Britain long before the mass migration movement of the late 1940s onwards.[17] This mass migration reached its peak in 1961 when approximately 74,590 entered this country. The year 1961 is significant, for it was one year prior to the 1962 Commonwealth Immigrants Act which greatly limited Black immigration from the Caribbean to Britain.

It is not my intention to spend a great deal of time repeating the sociological and historical reasons for the disproportionately large presence of Black people within the inner-city areas of Britain. By way of a brief summary, I feel it worth quoting Ceri Peach who states:

> The trend then, as now, is for White workers to move out of the large cities and industrial areas to new towns, suburbs and semi-rural areas. The Black population moved towards the inner city areas and the industrial towns to replace them.[18]

The African-Caribbean population in Britain has grown steadily from the comparatively small figures of the immediate post-war period through the peak figures of 1971.[19] It is estimated that around 28,000 people of African-Caribbean descent lived in Britain in 1951, whereas peak figures for this ethnic group are believed to be around 550,000 in 1971. Balarajan and Bulusu[20] are of the opinion that figures for African-Caribbean people in Britain have remained constant around the half a million mark since 1971. The growth over that time has been largely through natural increase.

The presence of African-Caribbean peoples in Britain can be explained by a number of factors. One significant phenomenon is the social and economic disruption experienced by Britain after the upheavals and traumas of the Second World War. In order to repair the damaged infrastructure of the British economy it was necessary to supplement a depleted workforce with increasing numbers of African-Caribbean migrants.

African-Caribbean people and historic-mainline churches

The churches within this study represent the larger historic-mainline churches in inner-city Birmingham. It would be foolish to suggest that the churches in question represent an exhaustive collection of all the Christian faith communities present in these particular settings.

The great majority of Black people to be found within these churches come from the Caribbean. Heather Walton, in detailing the historic-mainline links Methodism has had with the 'West Indian' islands, contends that almost three-quarters of Black Methodists trace their recent ancestry to the Caribbean.[21]

Renate Wilkinson identifies the majority of Black people from the Caribbean worshipping in the Anglican Church in Birmingham as originating from Jamaica.[22] The next largest group of Black people in the Anglican Church is from the Leeward Islands and Barbados respectively. The figures highlighted by Wilkinson are in many ways a concentrated picture of the larger social and cultural issues that reflect African-Caribbean migration and settlement patterns in Britain. Analysing the 1991 census, Peach states that:

> Jamaicans form the majority of the Caribbean-born population (54%), with Barbadians at just below one tenth of the population and Guyanese and Trinidadians just behind them. The Windwards and Leewards . . . as a rough estimate, about a third of the 'other Caribbean' category.[23]

Inner-city historic-mainline churches: central features and identity

The churches in which Black people worship vary enormously in size and complexion. There are many common issues and related factors, some of which I will describe in the following pages. At the outset, however, it is instructive to note that we are not describing a homogeneous grouping of churches with shared notions of community and solidarity. Rather, each separate worshipping community is an individual entity in its own right, with all the peculiarities and tensions one could expect to find in an individual church.

Some of the churches are large, both in premises and membership. Others are more modestly endowed. Some are extremely active in the area of community action, dialogue and involvement. Conversely, many inner-city churches would see such engagement with the local community as an anathema and superfluous to the ongoing life and witness of the church. Many of the churches will have ageing congregations, while others may be awash with young people.

It is the case, however, that there are many common features and issues to be found amongst inner-city churches. All of these faith communities exist in multi-ethnic, multi-faith and multicultural areas. Situations where issues such as unemployment, poor housing, disaffected youth (particularly within Black and Asian communities), inadequate public services, alienation from 'mainstream' society and racism are prevalent. Tony Holden reminds us that one of the results of the 'New Right's' ideological commitment to monetarism in the 1980s is the remorseless disparity between rich and poor most painfully manifested in the lives of people living in the inner-city.[24]

Clarice Nelson extends this point by reminding us that legislation enacted by successive Conservative administrations had a profound and disproportionately negative effect upon Black people in the inner cities in Britain.[25] Nelson continues by stating that the continued erosion of local authority power by central government has led to a subtle diminution in the effectiveness of the 1976 Race Relations Act. Given that this act was one of the few explicit attempts by the state to acknowledge and enshrine a mechanism for confronting institutionalized racism, this effect could be seen to have worrying, even grave, consequences.[26]

In many respects life within these inner-city faith communities reflects all the social and political developments that have had a marked effect upon the urban situation since the 1960s. Structural changes in the British economy gave rise to a host of social problems. Amongst the worst aspects were the spiralling levels of unemployment, the flight of the White middle class from inner-city areas, the crumbling of the infrastructure, and the fragmented sense of community and cohesion.[27] These factors have taken their toll upon, and have manifested themselves in, the life of these inner-city churches.[28]

The legacy of the past thirty years within inner-city areas has been the emergence of a desolate landscape, in which the presence of the once proud historic-mainline church continues to battle against seemingly impossible odds in order, in the first instance, to retain a sense of continuity with the past.

The present and future battles represent a more serious challenge, namely, to find new meaning in a continually evolving situation where the church is often perceived as being irrelevant. It is in these marginalized and self-contained worlds that the majority of Black youth find meaning and exercise their faith.

The historic-mainline churches have developed a variety of innovative responses and strategies. These responses have attempted to address the inherent, ongoing problems of their faith communities situated in inner-city areas. There have been a number of influential reports highlighting the endemic nature of racism within British society and inside the church.[29] The sharp disparity, however, between the high-flown rhetoric of well-intentioned reports and the continuing brutal realities of Black life in Britain is illustrated in Elton Lewis's 'Redemption Song'.[30]

The preponderance of church reports in the 1980s and early 1990s offered no lessening of the continued struggles of Black denial, pain and marginalisation in British society and within the church. The painfully honest dialogue between Clarice Nelson and Sybil Phoenix is testament to the continuing struggles of Black Christians to find their redemption and selfhood within the church and the wider society. A struggle that has yet to prove successful![31]

Black religiosity and White orthodoxy

Discussions with ministers, priests and curates of the churches within the study have revealed a portrait of church life in a state of evolution. The numerical ascendancy of Black people in these churches has mirrored the social and economic changes of the surrounding community. The changes in these churches have had a consequent impact upon the nature of church life in these distinct settings.

There is a wide disparity between White, European forms of worship and their accompanying cultures, and the linguistic traits and cultural forms of expression of African and Caribbean people. This difference represents some of the inherent tensions between two vastly different worlds of religious experience.

Gayraud Wilmore makes it clear that the religious experience of Black people and the expression of that experience find their origins in Africa.[32] The nature of Black peoples' religious expression has been in part a product of the resistance to White authority and oppression. This resistance first found expression in the system of slavery and the less overt expressions of power during colonialism.[33]

The development of this religious experience, says Wilmore, has been forged in the furnace of an ongoing struggle for truth. This tension is one between survival of present suffering and a hope for the future: a hope grounded in the notion that, in the end times (*eschaton*), full redemption for the oppressed and the marginalized will be realized. Black people the world over have held together these two aspects of experience as the primary means by which they find meaning and hope in a world of oppression of the poor and of people of colour.[34]

The formative experiences that have given rise to this distinctive form of religiosity stand in marked contrast to White, Eurocentric expressions of faith. The latter expressions tend to predominate within most historic-mainline churches in the inner-city and within Britain as a whole.

Black youth and questions of identity

An important issue that is often hidden, but remains a vital concern when discussing the Christian education of Black youth, is the issue of Black identity. It is important that commentators are conscious of the individual struggles of Black people to define and embrace their Blackness. Without such awareness there is, I believe, limited scope for a clear and precise understanding of the necessity for a specific, Black, African-centred model of Christian education. One must create strategies and teaching methods that assist Black people in their knowledge of self and the factors that have shaped their existence and experience.

As Clarice Nelson accurately surmises, the discovery of Black selfhood is primarily an exercise in justice, and as such, is a theological task. She writes, 'This greater voice of protest is yet to come about and will, probably, not come until a theology, a Black Theology relevant to the Black British situation, is developed.'[35]

The importance and necessity for Black theology and its relevance to Christian education, particularly as this discipline relates to Black youth, will be explored more fully in the second chapter of this book. At this point it is sufficient to say that Black theology has been of immense importance to this work. Black theology has served as the essential theological tool and the starting point for the struggle to create a new model for the Christian education of Black people in Britain.

One of the inherent difficulties in attempting to understand the nature of the identity crisis amongst Black youth is the danger of seeing their condition as being abnormal. This tendency to view Black youth as if there is something wrong with them often leads to particular roles being imposed upon this section of British society. Roles that are based on the often unspoken assumption that deviancy and dysfunctional behaviour are inextricably bound up with Black youth. Odida Quamina has commented on this tendency in his analysis of the media and its treatment of Black people.[36] This tendency to demonize Black people is not a new phenomenon. Writing over twenty-five years ago, Hartman and Hubbard commented on the pernicious nature of the media's treatment of Black people. The authors referred to the ways in which newspapers tend to report only the negative aspects of Black life in Britain. This negative form of representation is based on particular forms of social construction in which Black people are presented as essentially the problem.[37] Similarly, with notions of identity crisis amongst Black youth, one must resist the alluring temptation to use such sociological and cultural theories to attack Black youth.

Theoretical assumptions behind ideas on identity

Erikson in his seminal work on identity crisis amongst youth is at pains to detail the assumptions that arise from what is often a pejorative term.[38] Erikson contends that our understanding of what one might term an identity crisis should be seen as something that is normative and part of a general development of the intellectual processes of knowing.[39]

When young people are unclear of their place and role in society, one would expect them to go through what some term an 'identity crisis.' The word 'crisis' in this context should not be taken to mean any fatal or alarming catastrophe, but should be seen as normal. Clinically speaking, 'crisis' denotes a necessary turning point when the individual is in the process of trying to secure a new role and sense of belonging within the wider society.

This delicate process of identity formation can be exacerbated by a number of telling factors. One such factor is the additional burdens imposed upon those young people whose dominant family and cultural affiliations are not those shared by the majority. Freud calls this the 'Compact Majority'.[40]

Erikson, in particular, is most notable for the detailed work he has undertaken in the field of 'identity', with specific reference to the identity formations and crises of adolescents. In his writings, Erikson chronicles the various stages of the individual's development, and the increasing importance of the 'Ego identity', a term borrowed from Freud. 'Ego identity' relates to the conscious knowing self of the individual. It is that part of our make-up of which we are aware. 'Ego identity' is the awareness of the fact that there is a selfsameness and continuity to the ego's attempts to construct meaning for the individual. By this I mean that the conscious part of our mind is attempting to make sense of the world and to find a coherent pattern to the external world that confronts the individual. Coupled with this is the style of one's individuality, which is linked crucially to the style that coincides with the sameness and continuity of meaning for significant others who are in the wider community.[41] To put this in more basic terms, one's identity is not only constructed by the individual, but is influenced also by one's relationship with others. In other words, the 'group' as well as the 'self' influence the construction of the identity of an individual.

A good deal of Erikson's work rests upon the pioneering research and practice of Sigmund Freud. Freud, speaking of his own sense of identity as a Jew in Austria after World War One, described himself as slowly becoming aware of the attractions of his Jewish identity and of being a Jew. This awareness for Freud was a consciousness of his inner identity and the perception that he owed the basis of his character to his 'Jewish nature'.[42]

The question of identity, so fundamental to human beings and their mental construction, can be understood and expressed in a variety of ways. William James, in the course of writing to his wife, describes his identity in the following terms:

A man's character is discernible in the mental or moral attitude in which, when it came upon him, he felt himself most deeply and intensely active and alive. At such moments there is the voice inside which speaks and says 'This is the real me.'[43]

One may, for the sake of simplicity, describe the 'identity crisis' as a moral, intellectual and emotional attempt to discover and locate the real 'me' in the formation of one's natural self. This natural self is related to the wider environment of which one is a part, and is formed with reference to significant others.

The struggle for Black identity

It can be argued that identity crises understood with reference to our previous thinking do not remain the preserve of Black youth. Rather, they represent a perennial dilemma of many Black people, irrespective of age. This psychological struggle has its origins in the great upheavals of the Atlantic slave trade. The era of slavery was followed by a period of reconstruction and various acts of emancipation, and by the period of colonialism, that had so many recent echoes in the middle of the twentieth century.[44]

One of the major legacies of the era of slavery was the conscious and reasoned creation of an economic system that justified captivity. This was achieved through a rigid ideology that asserted the inferior status and subhuman nature of the African slave.[45] This form of insidious indoctrination was so pernicious that, to quote the notable reggae singer Bob Marley, it was a form of 'mental slavery'.[46]

The effects of such biased and self-serving instruction are still being felt – the continuing tendency of Black people to internalize their feelings of inferiority, coupled with an accompanying lack of self-esteem. This has led to Black people directing the fire of their repressed and denied selves onto themselves and those of their peers with whom they share a common ancestry and ethnic identity. Frantz Fanon describes the aggression shown by colonized and repressed people towards their peers and members of their own clan or ethnic grouping. Conversely, argues Fanon, greater insults can be levelled at these people by those who are oppressing them with comparatively little response from the individuals concerned.[47] The picture Fanon paints is reminiscent of the metaphor of crabs stuck in a barrel, fighting one another, rather than cooperating in order to challenge the oppressor who placed them in the barrel in the first place.

Erikson, writing from a clinical, Freudian perspective, poses an idea of the self-denied identity and repressed personhood in a manner that finds echoes with the assertions of Fanon. He, like Fanon and many others, recognizes the psychological damage that has been unleashed upon, and which continues to plague, the identities of people of African descent. Erikson writes:

> Therapeutic as well as reformist efforts verify the sad truth that in any system based upon suppression, exclusion and exploitation, the suppressed, excluded and exploited unconsciously accept the evil image they were made to represent by those who are dominant.[48]

As far back as 1903, the noted African-American intellectual W. E. B. Dubois highlighted the ongoing malaise within the warring soul of Black people.[49] Dubois termed this malaise 'Double Consciousness'. This struggle is a dialectical one – a struggle for ultimate truth between competing notions of reality. In the first instance there is the internal vision of the individual that is positive and clothed in the garment of belonging and self-affirmation. In short, the Black self knows it is important, for it is a conscious being and can, through interaction with others, gain a sense of its own value and worth. This internalized vision is juxtaposed with the external world of White authority and power, in which that same Black self is denigrated, demonized and disparaged. These two 'unreconciled strivings'[50] have continued to struggle within the battlefield of the Black mind.

There are a number of important issues relating to notions of identity that affect the children of the African diaspora living in post-colonial Britain. One of the primary challenges is the sense of having to contest one's identity and sense of space within White-dominated, post-colonial Britain in which the politics of belonging has been located within very narrow boundaries.[51] This process of negotiation has been in evidence since our earliest times in this country. In short, since our forebears were plucked from the ancestral cradle of Africa and transplanted to the Caribbean and the Americas, the past five centuries have been a perpetual and substantive struggle for self-definition. A search for a sense of identity that has not been dictated and imposed by White authority and White power.

The historical dimension

The search for a positive self-identity and the difficulties experienced by Black youth in their identity crises must be placed within a wider context. A context that is informed by the social, cultural and historical frameworks that have governed Black and White relations for six centuries. Winston James writing on Caribbean slave societies explains at length the disastrous effects that emerged from the widespread sexual liaisons between White slave masters and their Black slaves.[52]

A direct consequence of these sexual liaisons was the creation of an all pervasive 'multi-layered pigmentocracy'.[53] This term refers to the place of the individual in a society, and how that place was dictated by their shade of skin and the close affinities (or otherwise) with the facial characteristics most associated with White Europeans. Higman writes of eight such categories of skin pigmentation existing in the British colonies, ranging from 'Negro'[54] through to 'Octoroon'.[55] Remarkably, in the Spanish Americas there existed no fewer than 128 such categories.[56] James, commenting further on this phenomenon, has stated:

> Those who approximated most closely to the European type (in terms of hair texture, skin colour, facial characteristics, etc) were accorded high status (which almost invariably corresponded with their location within the class structure of society), and those who were deemed to have been without, or with few such characteristics, were likewise relegated to the bottom of the social hierarchy.[57]

Black people continue to internalize negative self-images of Blackness. This remains one of the primary difficulties for Black people in general, and Black youth in particular, as they seek to create identities which provide a positive self-image. One of the most eloquent commentators on this issue is the great Walter Rodney. Rodney points to the heart of the problem: 'But we continue to . . . express our support of the assumption that White Europeans have the monopoly of beauty, and that Black is the incarnation of ugliness.'[58]

Contemporary issues

The struggles of Black people in the diaspora over the previous six centuries, it can be argued, have become distilled within the individual experiences of Black youth living in post-colonial Britain. The sense of displacement, disaffection and marginality that exemplifies life for many Black young people living in Britain today is in many ways typified by Caryl Phillips in his book *The European Tribe.*[59]

In an early passage in the book, Phillips recalls a painful experience from his childhood. In a classroom discussion focusing upon identity of pupils derived from the surnames of all class members, his surname 'Phillips' becomes the butt of classroom humour. The humour that envelops the class arises from the patently obvious fact that Phillips is *not* perceived as being Welsh as his surname would seem to imply. 'Race', nationality and identity are seemingly at odds in this classroom incident. Phillips is not perceived as being one of them. The other White pupils are able to derive some sense of identity from their surnames. One boy is called Greenberg and is Jewish, while another boy called McKenzie is Scottish. Phillips, meanwhile, finds himself rootless and is exposed to the merciless taunts of his peers. Phillips writes, 'The truth was I had no idea where I was from as I had been told that I was born in the Caribbean but came from England. I could not participate in the joke, which made my identity a source of humour.'[60]

Consistent with and directly related to the search for a positive self-identity has been the sense of detachment and exclusion that has been keenly experienced by many Black young people in Britain.[61] In crude notional terms, Black young people, most of whom were born in Britain, are denied a rightful place within society because they do not *look* British.

According to Paul Gilroy the 'New Right' has refined the complexities of nationalism and identity into a simplified definition of Britishness.[62] The result is that an oversimplified and over-romanticized rural idyll of civilized 'Englishness' dominates the awareness and thinking of the nation. Britishness, which can and should be a broad, inclusive idea, has instead become a closed one, aligned in a narrow fashion to the rural White landed elite, who are often seen as synonymous with the establishment. In this case, this is often the established church, Oxbridge, the civil service, the army and of course, the aristocracy.[63] Black urbanized youth are excluded from this picture of Britishness.

In popular culture, this oversimplification of a romanticized England has been revealed in one of the most popular British films to be made in recent times – *Four Weddings and a Funeral*. In this film, the realities of urban, inner-city life, with its conspicuous multiculturalism and pluralistic nature, were ignored. Black people had no place in this sanitized version of Britain: a Britain created for public consumption in the international market place, particularly the United States. Is it any wonder then that many African-Americans are puzzled and surprised when they come face to face with Black people residing in Britain? They are amazed that Black people live in Britain. Notwithstanding the insularity and short-sightedness of many North Americans, in their defence one can cite the almost total invisibility of Black people in British films, especially in those that are aimed at the American market. The follow up to *Four Weddings* was in many respects even more scandalous. While one might argue that the context in which *Four Weddings* was set would quite naturally lead to the invisibility of Black presence (because we do not live in such areas, so it is argued?), *Notting Hill* was just grossly offensive and without excuse. Black people have lived in this area of west London for the past half a century. The biggest street party in the world has taken place there every August since the early 1960s. So how could our absence be explained, except on grounds that our presence is not conducive to the carefully polished image of Britain that the producers of *Notting Hill* wish to project to the world?

The Black response

The past twenty-five years have witnessed a variety of strategies adopted by Black youth to come to terms with life within British society. At its most basic, Black youth have sought to locate an identity within the communitarian ethic or the notion of community-based solidarity.[64] The late 1960s and 1970s saw the development of many informal and more formal Black organizations and groupings. The solidarity of shared experiences formed the bonds of this collective and corporate response. Writers from that period in contemporary British history have written extensively on this phenomenon.[65]

Contemporaneous accounts can be found in the work of Cashmore, Troyna and Pryce. Writing from the early 1980s Ernest Cashmore is at pains to remind us that the community-based struggles of Black youth should not be seen in purely passive terms. Throughout the 1970s, Black youth came together for purposes of mutual support, not simply as a response to their exclusion, but on their own pro-active terms – a recognition of the shared *positive* identity in their Blackness, and an emotional and psychological realization of their African heritage.[66] Cashmore emphasizes this point by saying:

> As young Blacks became aware of their colour and realise that it can be deprecated and used as a basis of exclusion, they fuse their Blackness with a new significance, incorporating it into consciousness, organising their subjective biographies so as to include it, strike up allegiances and perceived adversaries on the understanding of it. In general, positioning themselves in relation to that quality of Blackness.[67]

Perhaps the most striking example of this community-based

solidarity, and self-identifying ethic that gained great currency in the 1970s, is the Rastafarian movement. Pryce describes Rasta philosophy as being a mixture of mythic religiosity, superstition and African nationalism. With its distinctive rejection of Eurocentric concepts, Rastafari has given rise to an anti-establishment stance that is a form of resistance. More recently, William David Spencer has written a groundbreaking study, which traces the development of Rasta thought, with particular reference to the discipline of Christology (the study of Jesus Christ).[68]

The growth and popularity of the Rasta movement can be attributed to the sense of belonging and identity it conferred upon its adherents. The struggles and travails of life in 'Babylon'[69] (the exile of the African diaspora is equated with the Hebrew people in the Hebrew Scriptures more popularly known as the Old Testament) were validated, given meaning, and perhaps, of greatest import, offered vestiges of a future hope and a promised deliverance from bondage. This hope provided the emotional framework not dissimilar to the future hope (eschatology) provided by Black Christianity. Eschatological hope, with its focus upon the 'end times', turns present suffering into a temporary prelude when compared to the glorious 'final act' that will follow.[70]

Rastafari as a movement of cultural and political protest became a potent symbol for the alienated mass of disaffected and marginalized Black youth in 1970s Britain. It made Black youth feel they had a legitimate place in society, and gave them the confidence to reject the status quo and the biased self-serving thoughts of mainstream society. Moreover, it gave comfort and justification to the distinctive otherness of Black identity and experience.

The allure of Rastafari for many Black youth rested on what it *did not* represent. This in turn was placed alongside the positive ethical stances that personified the movement. Rastafari exerted a huge influence upon significant numbers of Black youth in the 1970s and early 1980s. Rasta philosophy is imbued with a positive identification of Africa as the ancestral homeland. This, coupled with the essential belief in the concept of 'Black' as a positive identity to be cherished, provided many Black young people with their first sense of self-esteem and pride.[71]

The movement had its many critics. Despite the many inherent flaws in Rasta ideology, Rastafari played a pivotal role in the development of a positive self-identity for many Black young people. Rasta philosophy provided the first ideological and representative tools by which the age-old insecurities and demonised approaches to education that had long shackled the children of the African diaspora could be dismantled.[72]

Afrocentricity, Black nationalism and Black youth in Britain

The Rasta movement may be seen as part of a larger Afrocentric or even Black nationalistic trend that became a significant movement in 1970s Britain. This continuing trend has sought to identify with African history and cultures that are a part of Black experience. These social, cultural and political movements led to an attempt to develop a Black hermeneutic or interpretative framework: one that asserted the prime importance of those traits, characteristics and forces that might be described as being quintessentially African.[73] This movement uses the African experience and the cultures that are reflected in the lives of Black people as the main source for interpreting the world and constructing ideas about what is 'truth'.

This burgeoning trend has given birth to a number of forms, from the neo-cultural and religious Black nationalism of the Nation of Islam,[74] through to the more socio-political stance of Pan-Africanist groups. Paul Gilroy has termed such nationalistic tendencies in their many guises as *essentialist*.[75] Gilroy is not taken with the seemingly simplistic identifications with Africa. He contends that essentialist notions of the *motherland* have a basic inability to deal in an honest fashion with contemporary Africa and the endemic problems which afflict that continent. Their proponents tend to romanticize the history of Africa, particularly the era that predates slavery. This period is seen as the glorious antiquity of the African people.[76]

Gilroy places the search for identity by Black youth in a much wider context than the seemingly simple recourse to African nationalism and the emotional language of Black people being 'family'. His approach to identity requires that Black identity, in its diversity, acknowledges the pluralism of the African heritage and its links with the forces and factors that recognize the r-o-u-t-e or the diasporan journeys of African people in addition to the r-o-o-t.[77] The latter r-o-o-t represents the African continent and the heritage that underpins one's notions of being an African person in the diaspora. In short, Gilroy is arguing that the Black Atlantic, the scene of the migratory journeys taken by Black people from Africa to the Americas and then to Britain, is the most important way of seeing and understanding Black identities in this country. This r-o-u-t-e is more important that the r-o-o-t (or origins) of Black identities that reside in and emerged from Africa.

Tony Sewell, writing about Black boys in British county schools, analyses the limited perspective held by Black nationalism with reference to notions of identity. Sewell challenges this perspective for its refusal to break dramatically with philosophical images of Africa as espoused by nineteenth century European romanticism.[78] Sewell, like Gilroy, argues for a more pluralistic notion of Black identities that are greater than the seemingly homogenous constructs of an African-centred approach – an approach that asserts that all Black people are the same and should think and behave in similar ways also.[79]

In the context of identity formation of Black youth in Britain, popular culture in general and music in particular are important sources, worthy of investigation. There are a wide variety of musical genres that play an important role in the identity formation of Black youth. These include ragga, jungle, rap, house, garage and rare-groove, in addition to older forms such as lovers' rock and reggae. Knowledge of these forms has helped cultural commentators, anthropologists and sociologists gain insights into the linguistic and rhythmical themes that imply a sense of identity amongst Black youth.

Les Back has undertaken an important study of modern youth in South London. He argues that the ongoing vibrancy of Black popular culture (particularly music), with its fluidity of expression and its acknowledgement of multiple sources, has enabled Black youth in Britain to locate a hybrid identity. This self-conscious hybridity or mixed identity addresses positively the identity crises amongst Black youth in Britain. Black youth are finding their identity in the multiplicity of musical genres that form Black popular culture.[80]

Back argues that the language of music located within the wider context of popular culture acts as a barometer for plural identities in modern youth. Paul Gilroy details the musical improvisational techniques and evolution that transformed a popular 1960s soul record beloved of many Jamaicans into an urban British classic. This process, argues Gilroy, serves as a metaphor for the complex and diverse processes that are in evidence in the creation of a whole new set of identities that are present in modern day Britain.[81]

There is much in this argument that I find persuasive. I am inclined, however, to retreat for one moment before examining the necessary and joyful improvisation that gave light to the synthesized final product. In order to describe my own counter-argument as a critique of Back, Gilroy and others, I would like to introduce a contrasting musical metaphor. I hope this metaphorical example will substantiate my point in a satisfactory manner. This metaphor is taken from jazz music.[82]

In jazz music the abilities of the musician to improvise, reform and transform a melody are rightly applauded. However, the melody remains the basis upon which all future performances and improvisations are based. I view this metaphor as a signifier for Black identities in post-colonial Britain. In jazz music, the great musicians are able to improvise upon the given melody, exploring new ideas, phrases, themes and even styles of playing. In fact, the very nature of how one plays the music, and with what intention or commitment, is challenged by the jazz musician. The melody may not sound anything like the traditional, inherited version. The purists may scoff in derision.[83] For example, the advent of be-bop in the 1940s brought torrents of abuse from the traditionalists of the swing era that preceded it. The newly improvised melody may sound nothing like the earlier versions that emerged before it. Yet it is the case that jazz musicians, in order to improvise on the inherited melody, must know something about the original version that came before them. One cannot improvise in a vacuum!

The metaphor of jazz music offers us a helpful way of seeing the relationship between the r-o-o-t and the r-o-u-t-e. I see huge significance in the many African-Caribbean cultural forms, traditions and examples of spirituality that have emerged. These elements provide the bedrock upon which all future identities for Black young people living in Britain can be built, and from which future ideas of self can be derived.

I believe we need to celebrate the r-o-o-t as a vital source and location of Black identity in Britain rather than simply relying on the r-o-u-t-e, which is implied in present notions of Black popular culture and the need to mix cultural forms. In the identity formation of Black youth, there is a need to reform, refashion, reconfigure and improvise. Cultures are never static, and that must include, also, our ideas of Black identity. Each generation has to learn and find a way of playing the inherited melody in a manner that speaks to the realities of their contemporary experiences. The r-o-o-t, however, remains vitally important in providing the basic sense of belonging and is the focus upon which all subsequent identities can be built. This r-o-o-t in question remains the African heritage that unites all Black people of the African diaspora. One's identification with the r-o-o-t may be imaginary, speculative or even mythical, but we should not become hostages to literalism or pragmatism.[84] Realistic dreams, images and myths play an important role in the construction of individual ideas of self and associated notions of identity.

A focus upon one's heritage does not imply a diminution of one's capacity or allegiance to be British. Nor is it a lazy process of mythologizing or romanticizing one's past for some spurious notion of 'essentialist' Black supremacy. Rather, it is a restating of the origins, antecedents and diasporan journeys that give rise to one's sense of the 'self' or the creation of the autonomous individual. These, in turn, provide the framework for any future perceptions or ideas that influence the identity of the individual. In this respect, I am in agreement with Molefi Kete Asante who describes all people of African descent as being linked by a unitary experience of being African.[85]

It is this experience of being African, that is global and contextual, universal and particular, generic and specialized, which provides the intellectual, philosophical and theological under-scoring of this work. I do not believe that anchoring one's identity upon the transitory nature of popular culture provides a secure basis for Black youth. The necessary security for their self-esteem and faith journeys must be built upon firmer ideas than a total reliance upon mixed identities without any secure base or upon diasporan routes.

The development of Christian faith amongst Black youth (in fact all Black and oppressed people) cannot be separated from the notion of one's individual self-identity as a (Black) person. The former must not become a convenient excuse to attack or deny the latter. The process of teaching and learning within the context of Christian education needs to be allied to an African-centred idea of selfhood that elevates and cherishes the divinely sanctioned Blackness of the African child.[86]

The use of Black culture as a resource for the Christian education of Black youth

The importance of Black music in particular and Black (popular) culture in general lies in the central power of both mediums. Black music possesses an ability to imply a sense of identity, coupled with notions of ethnic or familial belonging. It is my basic argument that any model for the Christian education for Black people needs to be informed by the important resource of Black (popular) culture, with music playing an important role.

A.V. Kelly outlines three common definitions of the word 'cul-ture'. He argues that with reference to an anthropological or socio-logical understanding of the term, culture refers to all aspects of the life of a society or a set of people – their beliefs, customs, mores, traditions and practices.[87]

I am interested in exploring the role of Black culture as the barometer and a repository for the ongoing experiences of African people in Africa and in the other parts of the world. If we take Kelly's description as being normative, then we have in Black

culture (or to be precise, cultures), an index for the lifestyles, traditions and practices of African people.

In seeking to reflect upon the ongoing influence and resonance of
Black culture for the benefit of this study, we must be careful not
to invest this area of Black experience with notions of mythical
and romanticized power. Cultures should not be seen as distinct
material entities in and of themselves. Cultures are constructed by
human action and imagination.[88] To focus upon Black culture as a
material entity in and of itself (as if it has a static existence beyond
the experiences of the people who are constantly re-creating it) is to
run the risk of romanticizing Black culture. Such romantic myths
surrounding Black culture are often used to create some form of
spurious counter-hegemony over and against White Eurocentric
ideas. In other words, the people who want to put forward a romanticized idea of Black culture are doing so in order to assert a form of
Black superiority and power over White people and their cultures
and practices. While this form of counter-argument is tempting
(perhaps understandably so), it is nevertheless without a great deal
of academic or scientific backing, and is against the spirit of the
teachings of Jesus.

Where to begin the discussion?

At what point can we profitably begin a discussion of Black cultures? For those who adopt an Afrocentric or African-centred perspective, any discussion of Black culture must begin in the very
cradle of civilization, namely Africa. Cheikh Anta Diop in his
seminal book[89] argues that the origins of modern civilization lie
firmly in Black Africa amongst people of the Negroid 'race'.

The notion of Afrocentricity posits the case for a coherent sense
of an African perspective on the world. This remains as persuasive
to a more modern generation of scholars as the efficacy of African
retention did amongst an earlier generation of academics. Molefi
Kete Asante in his highly influential book *Afrocentricity* makes the
case for a branch of study that is:

Pan-Africanist in its treatment of the creative, political, and geographic dimensions of our collective will to liberty. It is a discipline which underscores the relationship of Black people from various parts of the world, and as such organizes our thoughts and ideas into a composite whole.[90]

In a later work, Asante refers to culture as an important component in the Afrocentric debate.[91] This culture, argues Asante, is manifested in a variety of forms depending upon context and location within the diaspora. It can be seen, however, as a common thread that unites African people the world over.[92]

Afrocentricity attempts to challenge the myths that have bedevilled both African people and the continent of Africa as a whole. Dubois as early as 1915 argued against the falsification of African history and the attempts by European historians to distort and discredit Africa.[93] Maulana Karenga, commenting on the need for African people to understand their history and achievements, states: 'In understanding human history as a whole, Africans can even more critically appreciate their fundamental role in the origins of humanity and human civilisation and in the forward flow of human history.'[94]

Afrocentricity has had a profound influence upon a number of writers and scholars in a wide variety of disciplines. There is a body of thought, however, that has offered a sharp critique of Afrocentricity. Gilroy finds the brand of Black nationalism propagated by Afrocentrists problematic and is less than convinced of the notion of continuity and commonality between differing locations.[95]

Stuart Hall is critical of essentialist thought that seeks to impose rigid categorizations on our notions of 'race' and ethnicity.[96] Seemingly simplistic recourse to notions of 'pure race' and 'nationhood' are spurious and ambiguous. These concepts are unhelpful as they locate notions of Blackness within a social, historical and romantic construct that is as much a stereotype as the false images of 'other' constructed by White Europeans.[97]

There are very real problems inherent within Afrocentricity. Nevertheless, it offers a critically important tool and framework for the task of developing an appropriate model or example for the

Christian education of Black youth in Britain. At the very heart of the concept of Afrocentricity is the crucial resource of Black culture. Any attempt to create a specific Christian education programme for Black youth needs to acknowledge and use this vital resource.

Black culture has been and continues to be a vital barometer of the Black experience. As Robert Beckford suggests, it is 'a means of expressing the concerns of Black existence. Black culture is therefore an important arena for understanding what it means to be Black in Britain.'[98]

Black culture features prominently in this study. Black culture has been the vital means through which the historical experiences, spirituality, political and religious dissent and the ongoing liberation struggle of Black people have been expressed. The importance of Black culture in linking identity and relatedness to notions of Blackness ensures that any theologian or social scientist must be conscious of this reality. Black culture has been used by a number of theologians and Christian educators in their work with Black youth, particularly, in the United States. The work of these transatlantic scholars will be the focus of the next chapter.

'Pioneers Along the Way': Developing a Black Christian Education of Liberation

In this chapter I offer a brief overview of studies on the Christian education of Black people. It outlines historic developments in the theory and practice of teaching the Christian faith to people of African descent. This task will be undertaken by means of a four-part approach:

- An introduction to the nature and development of a Black Christian education of liberation;

- An outline of the work relating to the use of the Bible in this approach to education and theological reflection, and an investigation into the major ideological and philosophical issues involved;

- A description of the secular education of Black children, illustrating how this area has been a resource for the study of the teaching and learning of the Christian faith for Black people;

- A review of curriculum materials for this discipline.

Motivation to act

When I first commenced this study a respected practitioner in the area of children's and youth ministries informed me that the task of creating a new Black Christian education of liberation for Britain was both impossible and undesirable. Impossible because Black

Christian education is not a recognized discipline (he was not aware of any studies or literature pertaining to Black people), and undesirable because current practices are sufficient for all children and young people, whether Black or White. I hope to refute these contentions in this chapter. Of greater importance, however, this study provided me with the inspiration and the stimulus to create a new African-centred practical theology of education and liberation for Britain.

Sources and location for a Black Christian education of liberation

Most of the work done on the Christian education of Black people in general, and youth in particular, comes from the United States of America. This reflects the historic, economic and ideological strength and influence of African-American theological and educational thought. The development of Black Christian education is due to Black responses to racial oppression. The main purpose of those who are involved in this is personal and corporate liberation. There are fewer books and programmes on this subject that have come from Africa (with the notable exception of South Africa), and this reflects, perhaps, the different context and experience of Black people in their 'ancestral home'. Within Africa, where Black people not only form the majority, but are also indigenous to that continent, the emphasis is on the affirmation and defence of traditional forms of religious and cultural expression and theological inquiry, rather than on Black liberation.[1]

It is not my intention to suggest that Christian education done by people of African descent remains strictly a North American affair. It can be argued that in every country where Black people have taught and learnt the Christian faith, the practice of African-centred Christian education has been in evidence. While African-centred approaches to Christian education have existed at the level of practice, relatively little has emerged from the Caribbean, Europe and Africa in terms of academic study and systematic theory.

I have chosen to use the term 'a Black Christian education of liberation' in order to reflect the dual concerns of this discipline. The term 'Black' speaks to the prophetic, liberationist aspects which identify with the concerns of the God whose mission to the marginalized and oppressed is exemplified in the life, death and resurrection of Jesus Christ.[2] This prophetic stance is ideological because it asserts a particular and specific world-view. That world-view is shaped by a commitment to the Kingdom of God – the reversal of existing social norms. The term also reflects the cultural, social and historical experiences and expressions of faith of African peoples in the varied locations in which the Christian faith is practised.

Black Christian education: its central features

Early pioneering efforts: the dialogue with Black theology

The development of appropriate Christian education curriculum materials for Black people owes much to the pioneering work of Olivia Pearl Stokes. In the late 1960s and early 1970s Stokes argued for the need for Christian education within the Black church in the United States of America to be informed by the discipline of Black theology.[3]

To make the case for a Black Christian education of liberation one first needs to understand what is Black theology, because it is the source and the substance of this particular approach to Christian education. To explain in shorthand terms, if theology can be described as 'God talk', then Christian education is the means by which 'God talk' is taught and learnt amongst Christian communities. The first point of departure for a liberationist, Black, African-centred approach to Christian education is Black theology.

Black theology as a discipline owes a good deal of its existence to the seminal work of James Cone, who may be described as the 'founding father' of Black theology. Cone used the struggle of the Civil Rights movement of the 1960s, and the growth in the notion of Black Power in the latter half of that decade, as resources for theological exploration. Cone sought to find ways in which one could unite the militant Black nationalistic aspirations of such proponents as Malcolm X, with the more integrationist, pietistic Christian pronouncements of Martin Luther King.

These two contrasting poles in the Black American experience, argued Cone, were the twin foci that stimulated his interest in the creation of a Black theology of liberation. The combination of the ideological tenets of Black Power with Christian theology enabled Cone to construct a philosophy that attempted to reconcile two differing but united goals: the desire for Black self-determination and the notion of Black selfhood that is loved by God and created in God's own image.[4]

Cone's Black theology arose from his intellectual struggle to understand the contextual experiences of Black Americans within that Civil Rights era and the ferment of the Black Power movement. He describes the exercise of Black theology thus:

> Black Theology is a theology of and for Black people, an examination of their stories, tales, and sayings. It is an investigation of the mind into the raw materials of our pilgrimage, telling the story of 'how we got over'.[5]

In an earlier book, Cone contends that the central force of Black theology is its concern with the essential striving of Black people to understand their individual experiences and existence in a hostile, racist world.[6] He argues that Black theology is a theology of liberation. It is a mechanism by which Black people can explore their individual existence in light of their experience and their historical relationship with the God who desires them to be free. Cone writes:

> The task of Black Theology, then, is to analyze the nature of the gospel of Jesus Christ in the light of oppressed Blacks so they will see the gospel as inseparable from their humiliated condition, and as bestowing on them the necessary power to break the chains of oppression.[7]

When Olivia Pearl Stokes argued for the necessity of Black theology to be the point of departure for Black Christian education, she was highlighting a basic conviction of Black existence, namely, that central to the development of a Christian religious experience is the individual and corporate reality of Blackness: the condition of being Black in the world. It is this reality of being 'Black' in the world which, I believe, provides the first important case for a specialized Christian education scheme of teaching and learning for Black youth living in Britain.

Stokes was keenly aware of the forces and tenets of Black theology when she argued that such a discipline offered an important theory for all religious educators. This resource provided new theological insights from which the Black perspective could be understood and interpreted.[8]

Of particular import is Stokes' analysis of the work of the Christian Education Project that ran from 1966 to 1973. This project was an initiative of the Department of Christian Development within the National Council of Christian Churches (NCCC). The purpose of the project was the promotion, development and interpretation of a Black church programme of Christian education. This ecumenical initiative represented one of the first attempts by Black Americans to construct a viable Black Christian education programme rooted within the context of the Black church in America.[9]

The developmental work of the Christian Education Project was publicized in the July/August 1971 issue of *Spectrum,* a Christian education journal.[10] This special issue was given over to a symposium on Black Christian education, detailing some of the work of the project. Writing as part of that symposium, Enoch Oglesby argues passionately for the necessity of Christian education within this context to engage with the liberationist impulse of Black theology.[11] Oglesby believes that Black theology offers an ideological imperative for Christian education. This imperative has a rationale based upon the dialogue between Black experience and the gospel of Jesus Christ. He writes:

> The major task of Christian Education is nothing less than an awareness of and a commitment to a perspective on the Christian ministry of the church which understands God's mission in the world revealed in Jesus Christ as being not simply one of pietistic

love, humility and long suffering; but one of judgement, justice,
of political, social and cultural liberation of the poor and dispossessed.[12]

It is important that the educative process for Black people incorporates the important facets of self-identity and Black pride. These
are essential components of any Black Christian education programme. As early as 1969, a symposium on Black identity and the
potential for the future was discussed in *Religious Education*,[13] a
major journal detailing the latest research and practice in the field of
Christian and religious education. Joseph A. Johnson Jnr stressed
the necessity for Black people to embrace their Blackness as an
aspect of their identity which should be cherished. Black people, he
contended, need to gain a love for their culture, heritage, spirituality and traditions.[14] Black people need to be conscious that
'The Black experience is the womb out of which the new destiny is
created.'[15]

Most of the other contributions to the symposium share similar
sentiments. The remaining articles, each addressing a different context and subject matter, explain clearly the fundamental importance
of positive self-identities and a developed sense of self-esteem for
Black people.[16]

Colleen Birchett has undertaken a historical overview of Christian religious education in the Black church from the period of
slavery through to the modern era.[17] Birchett contends that the
Black church was slow to identify the importance of Christian religious education programmes, particularly for lay people, over and
above the need for trained clergy. Christian education was given
such a low priority within the life of the church that any attempts to
construct self-contained strategies of education seemed far-fetched
and speculative.[18]

It was not until the Civil Rights movement of the 1950s and 1960s
and the advent of Black theology, argues Birchett, that the Black
church began to take the discipline of Christian education seriously.
There was a belated recognition that this practical, theological discipline was an area which required serious engagement and much-
needed funds.[19]

The importance of the Black church: the most authentic setting for a Black Christian education of liberation

The term 'Black church' features prominently in the writings of many African-American Christian educators. The term is used to described particular faith communities in the United States, in which Black leadership, culture, traditions, experience and spirituality represent the norm, and from which White, Anglo-Saxon traditions and expressions are absent. These churches are not confined to any one denominational or theological slant. In Britain, the Black church is still largely synonymous with evangelical, Black-majority Pentecostalism.[20] In the United States it cuts across the whole spectrum of ecclesiology and the multiplicity of settings in which Black life is experienced.

In the United States of America the Black church developed because of the racism of the established churches of White, European origin. The worshipping life of the churches displayed discriminatory practices, forcing Black people to leave and form their own churches. The denominations most commonly identified with the Black church are the African Methodist Episcopal Church (AME), the African Methodist Episcopal Zion Church (AMEZ), the Christian Methodist Church (CME), the National Baptist Convention Incorporated, the National Baptist Convention of America, the Progressive Baptist Convention and the Church of God in Christ.[21]

Andrew White argues that the Black church has played an indispensable role in the development of Black Christian education within the American context, because it was the place where Black experience and selfhood was affirmed.[22]

Lonzy Edwards, writing on the birth of the Black church, details the first tentative efforts by Black slaves in the United States of America to construct their own places of worship. These centres of worship sought to bring a sense of self-worth and self-identity to a dispossessed and dehumanized set of people. Edwards asserts that the first steps in the creation of a Black, African-centred approach to teaching and learning emerged from these somewhat unpromising origins.[23]

The central importance of the Black church to the practice and
theory of African-centred approaches to education does not only lie
in its cultural and social status within Black communities in
America. Some writers maintain that the Black church is the only
place where Black people can be their true selves.[24] The Black
church has provided a safe environment, separate from the dictates
of White norms and their accompanying value systems. It has
offered a space where Black expression and experience can flourish
and be celebrated, away from prying eyes of derision and contempt.

Lawrence Jones believes that the notion of 'hope', grounded in
the very fabric of the lived experiences of Black people, must be the
core of any programme of religious teaching.[25] Jones reminds us
of the crucial role that the Black church plays in the religious
experience of Black people. He states that:

> As virtually the only self-sustaining, continuing institution with-
> in the Black community, the churches were matrices of commu-
> nity life. Blacks learned, but are in danger of forgetting, that if
> they affirmed themselves in community they could survive any-
> thing the larger society might impose upon them.[26]

This emphasis upon the Black church as the chief place for the
Black experience of faith is due to a number of factors. In practical
terms, it recognizes the importance of the Black church for the
ongoing experience and religious expression of Black people in
America. The Black church continues to represent the main co-
hesive, social, political and cultural institution that has enabled the
survival and liberation struggles of Black people in America for the
past four hundred years.[27]

C. D. Coleman argues that the Black church represents the most
holistic expression of Black people themselves. It is the first and the
most successful model in collective strength and corporate identity.[28] Coleman continues: 'To its woebegone masses, the Black
Church gave realism and substance to things hoped for and the
undeniable evidence of things not seen.'[29]

James H. Harris reminds us that the Black church remains the
bedrock of the Black religious experience in the United States. Any
Black theological discussion that is not conscious of this reality and

does not seek to engage in a dialogue with the Black church will be condemned to irrelevancy.[30]

Riggins Earl Jnr speaks of the pivotal and unique role of the Black church within Black communities. From this favoured vantage point the Black church must be involved in the task of inculcating 'survival skills' into her young people, as an integral part of their Sunday school education.[31] William A. Jones argues that the Black church has provided the strong base from which challenges to the institutionalized racism of the American State could be mounted. This has been, and continues to be, the prophetic role of the Black church in the United States of America.[32]

Sunday school and the Black church

The role of the Sunday school has long been seen as the crucial setting in which the basic ideas of Black Christian education have been practised. Mary Love argues that the Sunday school within the Black church is highly influential in the Christian formation of African-Americans. The Sunday school assisted African-American slaves to reinterpret and subvert the biased, self-serving teachings of Christianity espoused by White slave masters. This subversive transformation enabled Black people to see Christianity not as the sole domain of the slave master, but as an instrument in the liberation of the African spirit.[33]

Love argues that the process of Christian education has had to be one of invention, imagination and improvisation.[34] Johnson reminds us that the Sunday school and the role of Christian education within the Black church were of paramount importance because the skills of survival were taught and learnt in these contexts.[35]

Harold D. Trulear argues that Christian religious education in the African-American tradition has been a struggle for identity and structure. He states that many Sunday schools grew out of ad hoc arrangements in situations where trained leadership was scarce and finance even more so. Many of these Sunday schools worked on a semi-autonomous basis with little effective guidance or control from the clergy.[36]

Black churches in Britain

Within the historic-mainline traditions in Britain the term 'Black church' cannot be seen as synonymous with an understanding that has emerged from the United States of America. Black churches within historic-mainline traditions in the United Kingdom have very different roots and development from their American counter-parts. Their development in the United Kingdom owes more to the demographic, socio-economic realities of inner-city Britain than to the religio-cultural experiences that have shaped African-American peoples in the United States. The Black church in the United States of America is inextricably linked to the cultural and theological expressions of faith of Black people. Within Black-majority churches in the historic-mainline traditions in Britain, the development of a theological framework for the exercising and the expression of Christian faith is still in its comparatively early stages.[37]

While one should be wary of simplistic and naïve comparisons between the differing understanding and forms of the Black church between the United States and Britain, there is much that can be learnt from our transatlantic cousins. The development and pro-gress of the Black church in the United States has provided a haven from the worst excesses of racial oppression. Apart from creating a safe hospitable space for African-Americans, the Black church has affirmed Black cultural and religious experience and expression. This affirmation and sense of belonging has led to many African-Americans developing increased levels of self-confidence, self-esteem, empowerment and economic self-determination.

In the following chapters I will outline the development and growth of African-centred perspectives on worship and learning, within a number of historic-mainline inner-city churches in Birmingham. These developments, the result of the implementa-tion of a newly created model for a Black Christian education of liberation, have provided the impetus for the emergence of Black churches. If this approach to Christian education is to become the norm in predominantly inner-city settings, then there will need to be an accompanying commitment to developing Black churches in

Britain – churches that reflect the cultures, experiences and expressions of faith of Black people of African descent.

There are many for whom this development would be an anathema. I would, however, point to the growth of such churches in the United States, and to the proliferation of Black-led Pentecostal churches in Britain. It is not my contention that one should strive to replicate these models, whether in the United States or in Britain. However, the success of these faith communities in reflecting and affirming the experiences and cultures of Black people (a major factor in their growth) cannot be dismissed lightly.

For those churches that might describe themselves as 'multi-ethnic', I would argue that incorporating a Black African-centred perspective on worship will not only energize and invigorate the whole church, but will also provide a liberationist perspective on the gospel, which will, ultimately, emancipate all people within the church.[38]

The influence of Grant Shockley: a prolific apologist for a Black Christian education of liberation

It can be argued that Grant Shockley[39] has been the most influential and prolific Black Christian education theorist and writer of the past thirty years.[40] Shockley's concern is that Christian education for Black people should be liberationist and transforming. Any programme must be concerned with social justice and be aligned to a biblically prophetic hermeneutic.[41]

He argued convincingly that the Christian education of Black people should be rooted in the concrete realities that inform the experience of the individual. Moreover, programmes and processes should offer tools and strategies by which their desire for freedom can be made real and concrete.[42] Shockley reminds us that the religious experience of Black people in many countries has been forged and developed in the furnace of oppression and marginalization.[43]

Shockley insists that Black Christian education should be contextual, liberating and relevant to the needs and realities of Black people. He emphasizes the need for such disciplines to be informed by the practice and theory of Black theology. He writes:

Black Theology has been instructive at the point of letting us know that any Religious Education programme that might be constructed, must grow out of and center around the experiences, relationships and situational dilemmas that Black people face in their day to day struggle to survive, develop, and progress in an often hostile, uncaring majority-dominated society.[44]

Shockley outlines what he considers to be imperatives for the Christian education of Black people. He argues that the Black experience provides the foundation upon which any strategy of teaching and learning and the content of Christian education should be based.[45] He presents an ideological framework in theological and educational terms. This approach envisages a radical reconfiguring of the present world order. Beginning with an analysis of the historical experiences of Black people, Shockley proceeds to outline the sociocultural foundations for a specific cultural teaching and learning strategy for Christian education.[46]

Shockley, like many of his peers, argues that the link between the processes of Christian education and the affirming reality of the Black church should be recognized and affirmed. He contends that this relationship should be used strategically for furthering the important task of liberation within Black communities across the United States of America.[47]

He argues against the inherent conservatism of many Black churches, which has led them to adopt an educational philosophy that is hierarchical, authoritarian, passive and wedded to the maintenance of the status quo. In order to correct this, he charts the new developments in Christian education in the Black church, and highlights the necessity for these influential centres of faith to align themselves with progressive movements in educational philosophy.[48] Shockley is anxious that a Black Christian education of liberation should reflect the latest thinking in best educational theory and practice.

Black Christian education between cultures and generations

There has emerged in the past twenty-five years a theory that has argued for an intergenerational process of education and nurture – what one might describe as a process of socialization into the cultural and religious environment of the Black church.

Perhaps the most influential figure in this development is Charles Foster. 'Inculturation' attempts to combine the corporate culture of a set of people, or an institution, with the ongoing narrative of the sacred texts and religious traditions which guide that community. By attempting to make their religious traditions culturally relevant, believers and learners are hoping to localize and recast their belief-structures into a form that speaks to their specific cultural environment and experience.

Foster, a White Christian educator, has been committed for many years to the cause of Black liberation.[49] He stresses the need for Black people, especially Black youth, to be educated into the worshipping, celebratory and learning culture of the church. Foster asserts that the life of the community of faith represents the ideal model in which individuals discover their identity, their sense of self, and a positive measure of affirmation. Foster states that:

> The life of the community is the content of Christian Education. Participation in its heritage, rituals, traditions and lifestyles, as well as thinking, values and institutions provides both the context and the content of the interaction between teachers and learners.[50]

Foster is not concerned solely with the importance of the whole community of faith participating in the educative task. He is aware of the subtle issues of power that often promote notions of exclusivity and superiority within seemingly homogeneous faith groupings. Foster warns against communities of faith perceiving their corporate life as being normative, i.e, 'being as it should be'. The corollary of this normative belief is the labelling of different ethnic and cultural groups as being 'other'.[51] Foster argues that faith communities need to engage with issues of multiculturalism and

differing perspectives within their Christian education programmes. This alternative focus is crucial, for it offers opportunities
to develop a growing appreciation of the importance of inclusivity
and the valuing of people from different ethnic backgrounds.[52]

Foster stresses that churches within multicultural societies must
adopt a double consciousness approach. This approach enables people to recognize different perspectives and traditions, while valuing
and affirming their own particularity.[53] He continues by claiming
that:

> A primary context for the Religious Education of persons in
> multicultural contexts occurs not in isolation of their cultural
> experiences in teaching learning activities or in the imposition of
> one cultural perspective over another, but at the intersection of
> their encounters with each other.[54]

This perspective is one which, if taken seriously, assists in refut-
ing any notion of 'reverse racism and discrimination' by acknowledging the multiplicity of experiences and cultures that are evident
in all faith communities. In response to the plurality of many
churches, Foster attempts to articulate the seeming tension inherent within many faith communities: the necessity, in the first
instance, to move beyond endemic insularity and exclusivity. The
alternative perspective in this dialogue for truth is the attempt to
unite people of all ages within a community of faith into an effective
appropriation of the stories and traditions that are a part of any corporate group of people. The second half of this dialogue, asserts
Foster, remains a critical task for every church. He writes, 'One of
the most critical tasks facing the church, then, has to do with the
effectiveness with which each successive generation appropriates
the story of its heritage and internalises the promises inherent in the
story.'[55]

Foster's commitment to a whole church, intergenerational and
intercultural approach to Black Christian education is crucial, for it
reminds us that the task of learning the life-changing truths of the
gospel cannot be separated from the rituals, liturgies and the corporate worship and celebratory life of the church. Any process of

Christian education which makes a permanent separation between learning and worship is providing a barely adequate and a very limited perspective on the nature of Christian formation and nurture. Within the Black Christian education programme and theory I have developed, worship and the wider life of the church are essential components in the overall teaching and learning strategy. This is emphasized in the following chapters.

Significant influences and concerns

Black Christian education and the Bible

The work that relates more specifically to the Christian education of Black people reflects the socio-political and theological dominance of the United States of America. Before we begin to explore the relationship between Black approaches to Christian education and the Bible, we need, briefly, to explore the basic philosophical approaches to the use of the Bible in the teaching and learning process. In order to do this, I will refer to the work of the religious education theorist, Harold William Burgess, who outlines three general methods of religious education.[56]

The first method is based on a transcendentalist view. It asserts that God is above and beyond the process of education. In this approach, the teacher's role is primarily didactic or instructional. This approach often views the Bible uncritically – the teaching and learning process is governed largely by the prompting of the Holy Spirit and the self-revelation of God, which, it is believed, is effected directly from Scripture without the need for any interpretation from either the teacher or the learner.

The second method is an immanentist strategy, although an alternative term that is often used is the liberal approach.[57] This approach poses the belief that God is within the process of teaching, not external to it. The presence of God and the activity and movement of the divine is found within social scientific theories for human growth and development. Lee asserts that religious education is primarily an educative task and, as such, social science provides the only valid overarching theory for this discipline, not theology. Lee is somewhat dismissive of the transcendentalist perspective on Christian education. He disparages the view that God is external to the educational process through the power of the Holy Spirit as the 'blow theory'.[58] The third method outlined by Burgess is a synthesis of the two previous methods.

This brief summary of the methods of religious education is important, for it offers us an overall framework within which the Christian education of Black people in Britain can be located. The development of Black Christian education in more recent times has tended to synthesize the transcendentalist or 'God above' and immanentist or 'God within' perspectives as outlined by Burgess. This synthesized approach accords, therefore, with the method that incorporates both poles of the teaching and learning continuum.

Milton Owens, writing on the links between the Christian education of Black people and the Bible, describes an approach that reflects the third method outlined by Burgess. Owens outlines an approach that attempts to link the experience of Black Americans with specific texts in the Bible.

Through a six-stage programme Owens attempts to assist African-American youth to understand the connection between the Bible and the historical and ongoing experiences of Black people in America. Using an activity-based approach to education, Owens encourages children and young people to be in active dialogue with their traditions, linking biblical texts with contemporary realities. He writes of this process: 'Our return to the attic has been an exciting event. We have begun to rediscover our heritage, our roots, our 'who we are'. In doing so we are beginning to discover our future and our priorities for the nowness of life.'[59]

My approach to the Christian education of Black youth has been influenced greatly by Owens' work. This approach uses the Bible as a direct resource for Christian education and is echoed in a more recent work by Joseph Crockett. He outlines a strategy that relies heavily upon narrative and interactive storytelling, which attempts to link African-Americans with the transforming power of the Bible.[60] Crockett highlights a number of themes linked to the historical and more recent experiences of African-Americans. One of the major themes developed in his work is the question of exile.

Exile, argues Crockett, has helped African-Americans' understanding of life. He writes:

> The theme of exile as a focusing lens for teaching scripture allows us as African-American Christians to be faithful to our history and experience. The exile serves as a reference in making sense of the dispersion of our ancestors from Africa.[61]

Cain Hope Felder, a renowned biblical theologian on the Hebrew scriptures, asserts the need for African-Americans to reinterpret the Bible in the light of their unique experiences. Felder argues that biblically-based studies must seek to engage with the various texts of Scripture in order to highlight an African perspective on our modern perceptions and misconceptions concerning what one might term biblical truth.[62] Felder is insistent that people of African descent must engage with the Bible in order to create a 'self-perpetuating liberation'.[63]

Keith Chism argues that Christian education should permit those engaged in the teaching and learning process to appropriate the stories of the Bible as their own stories. The form of appropriation is crucial to the contextualization relating to the life settings of biblical texts.[64]

In order to highlight the use of the Bible in Black, liberationist approaches to Christian education, I have included a brief Bible study to show how Scripture can be read critically in the service of Black liberation.

A Black liberationist Bible study

The method for this Bible study has been drawn from the extensive work undertaken by biblical scholars from the so-called 'Two-Thirds' world. Using many of the central ideas of Black, womanist and liberation theologies, these authors have attempted to create a distinctive approach to reading the Bible. This approach is one that emerges from the struggles and life experiences of the poor and marginalized. Writers such as Sugirtharajah have termed this approach 'post-colonial theology'.[65]

This Bible study is based upon Acts 8.26–40 – the story of Philip and the Ethiopian official.

Instructions

* Give the group a number of large sheets of paper (A4 prefer- ably) and ask them to draw a vertical line down the centre of each page. On the left-hand side of the paper, ask them to write down the word 'advantages'. On the right-hand side, they should write 'disadvantages'.

* Ask the group to respond to the following set of questions: (1) Who or what sort of people have the main advantages in the world? Write down your answers on the left-hand side of the sheet. Who or what sort of people have the disadvan- tages? Answers on the right. (2) The people on the left, where do they live? The people on the right, where do they live? (3) What kind of facilities do the people on the left have? (water, food, health care, education, etc.). What about the people on the right? (4) Who controls the world's resources and the financial markets of the world, the people on the left or the right? Who does not control these things, the people on the left or right? (5) Are the people on the left more likely to be men or women? What about the people on the right? (6) Are the people on the left most likely to be Black, Asian, Latino or White? What about the people on the right? *Now for the big questions. There are two of them! First (7) Which side of the line do you think you are on? Are you on the left or the right? (Honestly now! Look closely at the two different groups.) Second (8) Which side would you like to be on, the left or the right? Which side would the majority of the world like to be on?*

* Look at the two lists. Split the group into two halves. One half of the group are the people on the left-hand side of the sheet. The other half are the people on the right. Give each

group two or three minutes to consider what life is like being the type of person who is on the left- or the right-hand side of the sheet of paper.

- Ask the two groups to reassemble. What do they have to say to each other?

- What is the biggest difference between the two sets of people? Given your differences, do you think this will affect how you will see the world?

- It is obviously the case that the world can be divided up in many different ways. There are people who live in different countries. Across the world, people speak different languages, have different traditions or different cultures. From the exercise we have just completed, one important way in which the world can be divided is between those who have many advantages and those who do not. A world divided between rich and poor. Poverty comes in many different forms; economic poverty, but there is also poverty of spirit, poverty of hope and poverty of opportunity.

Reflections on the passage and the exercise

What is your impression of the Ethiopian official? With which person do you identify in the story, Philip or the Ethiopian official? This may seem like an easy, straightforward question, but it is quite a complex one if you pause to give it further thought.

In a number of biblical passages we see interesting encounters between people who appear to be very different. Naturally, as is the case in most stories, we are invited to identify with one person (and their perspective) rather than the other. In this story, it is often the case that Christian communities have traditionally identified with Philip. He, after all, is the apostle. He is perceived to be on our side. He is 'one of us'. The other person, in this case, the Ethiopian official, is not 'one of us'. He is the 'other'. The fact that he can be identified as a Black person perhaps makes it all the more difficult to see him as 'one of us'. His place in the story, so it would seem, is to enable Philip to preach a great sermon about Jesus. The Ethiopian official is not a person in his own right, but simply a cipher through which the gospel of Christ can be proclaimed by Philip.

After further reflection, some of you may have identified with Philip, an apostle of Jesus. He is a believer and is in possession of knowledge of the Scriptures. What about the Ethiopian official? What about him? Where is Ethiopia? Ethiopia is a country in Northern Africa. Many people have identified with the Ethiopian official for a number of reasons. Can you think of any? Some have identified with this man because he is Black and is a person of authority. He is an official in the Ethiopian royal court. Given the often stereotypical images we have of African people, often through the media, especially on the news, we would imagine that he is poor or badly educated. Yet this man is someone of importance.

In the world in which we live, the majority of the people who face disadvantage are Black, or people of colour who are not European or of European ancestry. Many of these people are often shown in a negative light, as individuals who can only be poor, with little or no education and having no importance. Yet, here in this story, we see someone from a background familiar to many of you. Can this man serve as an example to Black people? If yes, then how? It may be argued that this man can become a role model for disadvantaged people, many of whom have been in their situation for so long, they and others believe it is the only situation they know – that their situation is almost a natural one. Many disadvantaged people, particularly if they are Black, have read into this passage (taking their circumstances into direct consideration) a reminder that long before Europeans came to the African continent and enslaved many Black people, some of these people were important, noble and educated individuals. Black people do not necessarily have to be poor or badly educated or lacking in respect or to be pitied.

The Ethiopian official, if you are coming from a situation of disadvantage, can offer you a hopeful picture of what you could become.

This Bible study is based upon the important task of reading and re-reading the text (the writing in Scripture) in light of the experience of the person who is looking at the story. In this Bible study, I have used a Black interpretative framework (or hermeneutic) to read this passage of Scripture, in order that it might speak to the experience of Black people and be a source of support and encouragement.

The use of the Bible in a Black liberationist approach to Christian education will be explored in greater detail in the following chapter, where I will offer a more detailed exploration into the work I have undertaken in order to bring Black experience into dialogue with Scripture.

By way of a brief summation at this point, it can be stated that Black Christian education has distanced itself from the liberal versus conservative arguments concerning the role of the Bible in Christian education. The extreme liberal position, which has seen the Bible as purely an important resource (alongside many others of equal importance) in the Christian education of young people, is rejected. The ultra-conservative approach that sees the Bible as complete in and of itself, removed from contaminating dialogue with human experience and interpretation, is also rejected.

Ideological and philosophical issues within a Black Christian education of liberation

The work of Janice Hale: assessing the needs of Black youth

One of the most influential theorists and practitioners in the Christian and general education of Black children in recent times is Janice Hale (née Hale-Benson). She has written extensively on the educational needs of Black children, in both intellectual and emotional terms. She argues that educationalists need to be aware of the specific environmental factors that often reflect Black cultures, into which Black children are nurtured. These particular environments are separate and distinct from a dominant White, Anglo-Saxon perspective. These cultural environments, in turn, have given rise to Black children's specific learning styles, which need to be recognized and affirmed if effective teaching strategies are to be constructed for their learning.[66]

Hale asserts that culture shapes the intellectual process of knowing. While highlighting the seminal work of Piaget, she contrasts her own approach with that propounded by the Swiss developmental psychologist. Hale explains that the intellectual process of knowing is not only biological but also has a social and cultural dimension. By this, she means that the development of our human capacities for knowing arises through the natural growth of the human body. That is, from the moment we are babies our bodies grow and develop, as do our capacities to know. Hale argues that, in addition to this form of biological cognition or knowing, there is the important aspect of culture and the wider environment in which the individual lives, which also shapes one's ability to know. In light of this belief, the crucial element of cultural transmission needs to be understood, particularly in its effects upon biological and intellectual development.[67]

Hale extends this thesis by stating that Black children have distinct learning styles that differ from children of other ethnic groups. Drawing upon important research by Rosalie Cohen,[68] Hale outlines the means by which different patterns of nurture and development can have a profound impact upon the intellectual development and learning styles of children from a variety of ethnic groups. Black children, she argues, have their own unique styles of learning, styles influenced by particular patterns of nurture and care.[69] She believes that Black children are adversely affected by the existing norms and patterns of education evident in a number of western societies. These models, asserts Hale, favour the behavioural patterns and learning styles of children of White, European descent.[70]

In her follow-up to the highly influential *Black Children* she outlines the cultural and environmental influences that have given rise to the distinctive oral culture of Black people.[71] She argues that this distinctive and expressive quality, in addition to being affirmed, should become an essential component in any teaching and learning strategy and programme for the Christian and more general education of Black children.[72]

Linguistic and cultural issues in the education of Black youth

Hale believes that people of African descent possess particular speech patterns and culturally specific dialects. These patterns and dialects not only imply identity and cultural transmission, they are also an indication of the intellectual and emotional development of Black people.[73] They often find expression in traditional folktales and proverbs. Beckles reminds us that, within the educational system in Britain, insufficient credence has been given to the language needs and distinctive speech patterns of African-Caribbean children. These speech patterns are valuable in their own right and are not merely crude variants of Standard English.[74]

Questions related to the transmission of cultural values to children of African descent are important ones within the literature. Janice Hale states that the varied cultural traits within diasporan African life are the product of a dynamic interchange between traditional African religions and western Christianity.[75] An essential feature of cultural transmission amongst African peoples has been the efforts to socialize Black children into the philosophical worldview of their forebears. Exposure to this process provides these children with a sense of the historic developments that have played a significant role in the shaping of their identity.[76]

Janice Hale outlines a holistic vision for educating Black children in the context of the cultures and traditions into which they have been born and nurtured. It is her belief that any teaching strategy for Black children must be allied to their cultural practices, traditions, history, faith narratives and experiences of people of African descent.[77] Hale is insistent that education for Black children should possess high emotional support, coupled with the need to promote positive self-identity, while encouraging creative expression. This particular vision for education should be informed by Black history.

Empowering Black youth

One of the most important recent studies into the Christian education of Black youth has been undertaken by Michael Ross. The
central focus of Ross' research has been African American males.
Ross argues that effective Christian education must be formational,
helping young Black people, particularly young boys, to make the
transition into responsible adulthood. This teaching and learning
scheme is constructed in order that Black boys can gain a sense of
the historical legacy and the more recent developments in Black
masculinity. This educational process will assist such individuals to
discover identities that are informed by the legacy of faith of which
they are a part.[78]

An early advocate of the importance of the ideological intent of
Christian education with reference to Black youth was Helen
Archibald. She states that Christian education for such individuals
must 'Combat the poison they know lives about them.'[79] Archibald
goes on to say that 'Religion is that which interposes itself between
the bent back about to be broken and the whole crushing weight of
the world's evil and injustice.'[80]

The amelioration of contextual woes, as detailed by Archibald, is
also a concern of Andrew White, who states that Christian education under the auspices of the Black church must be a practical exercise in liberation.[81] White believes that Christian education should
introduce Black youth to the often disguised and suppressed mili-
tancy of Jesus, upon whom Christian teaching must be based. He
states that:

> Jesus was militant and a revolutionist who understood justice to
> have a specific and practical meaning. The young Blacks will
> identify with him if they are informed about his programme for
> peace, justice, brotherhood and equality, in practical observable
> actions.[82]

Nelson Copeland has written of the need for Christian education
to be conscious of and informed by the contextual realities of Black
youth culture. Copeland makes the case for a form of Christian education that is linked inextricably to the experiences of Black youth

and equips young people to develop the necessary tools for their own liberation.[83] The importance of encouraging and enabling Black young people to begin to locate appropriate solutions to their own problems is a theme to which Copeland returns at a later stage in his writing. He argues that Black young people should be empowered to reflect critically so that they refuse to accept superficial solutions, while continuing to pose hard questions.[84]

Copeland asserts that many Black young people no longer possess the capacity to reflect critically because they have lost the inherent self-belief that is often a prerequisite of that particular facet of human consciousness.[85] This theme is echoed in the work of Na'im Akbar. Commenting upon this psychological deficiency amongst Black people, he refers to the term 'plantation ghost'. He claims that those struggling from this malaise are individuals who have been dehumanized and psychologically shorn of every shred of belief in their own abilities and self-worth. In effect these people have become brainwashed.[86]

There has been an increased emphasis in more recent times on the need for Black youth to gain a positive vision of their individual selfhood. Some, such as Useni Eugene Perkins, have argued that African people from previous eras possessed a number of advantages over their younger counterparts. African people from past epochs, although struggling with pernicious and overt racism, possessed a much clearer sense of their own self-worth and personhood.[87] This is due, in part, to the greater levels of autonomy experienced by Black people, in settings that were more overtly racist than many western societies at the present time. In short, if the enemy is less guarded in their hatred and animosity, there can be no doubting your position and standing in comparison to theirs. As a consequence, one is forced to develop practical strategies for countering such negativity. Conversely, if the enemy is more subtle, and even notionally sympathetic, one can be lulled into a false sense of security, consequently believing the myths of understanding and empathy, which may be illusory.

Perkins continues by reminding us that the continual denial of the Black psyche has led to many Black people believing the myths of their own inferiority. Perkins argues that education must assist

Black youth to see beyond the limitations conferred upon them by a discriminatory society. Black youth need to be empowered to envisage a future in which all distortions are challenged and scrutinised for their veracity.[88]

Michael Clarke's thesis for the Christian education of Black youth in the Anglican Church in Barbados is somewhat less strident than some of the models proposed in the United States of America. His work remains persuasive, however, not least for the contextual theological model he proposes for his own situation.[89] Clarke proposes a praxis model of Christian education – a model that calls for theory and practice, action and reflection to be held together in a unitary whole. This approach, in effect, is a model for a practical theology that attempts to engage Black young people with the historical dimensions of culture and faith that have, to a greater extent, been submerged and suppressed within that island.[90]

George Champion offers a less ideological model for the Christian education of Black people (with particular reference to young people). The approach proposed by Champion is instructional and prescriptive, utilizing rote learning and memory verses as a major part of the teaching-learning process.[91] His teaching and learning scheme, however, reflects many of the dominant themes in the literature, in that it asserts the need for Black youth to be introduced to the historical developments of faith of people of African descent. Particular emphasis is placed upon developing self-esteem and a strong sense of identity. Champion seeks to incorporate elements of African-American cultural traditions and practices into his teaching strategy and programme in order to assist African-American boys to gain a more positive sense of Black masculinity.[92] This method is similar in many respects to that used by Ross.

The secular education of Black youth: a resource for a Black Christian education of liberation

In reviewing the significant studies and theories pertaining to the Christian education of Black youth, I was conscious of the relatively small number of studies directed at young people per se when compared to more general studies of Black adults. A second observation concerned the location from which much of this literature comes, namely, the United States of America. As a corrective to the two previous observations, I have decided to devote the following section to exploring contemporary literature pertaining to Black youth that comes from a more general or secular perspective. Secondly, particular emphasis will be placed upon models or concerns that have arisen from the British context.

The rationale for this decision is twofold. First, I believe it is important to engage with James Michael Lee's assertion that Christian education is properly understood as a branch of education. Christian education should be governed by the tenets of sound educational practice and the norms of human development and learning.[93] I am not in total agreement with this argument and would, like my intellectual mentor Grant Shockley, consider myself to be a Black Christian educator and a practical theologian. For Shockley, Christian education is a theological discipline, influenced by our attempts to undertake constructive conversation concerning the God who calls us into a redemptive relationship with God's own self.[94]

In order to widen the context of this study, I have decided to use important findings from a variety of disciplines including sociology, psychology, cultural and literary theory and the philosophy of education.

In the second instance there is the overwhelming balance of the literature to which I have referred. These works have come from the United States of America. Given that this study is located in Britain, it is imperative that I investigate appropriate models of education that are located within the British context.

In looking at the general educational literature for Black youth, I am obliged to begin my assessment once more in the United States. One of the most influential writers concerning the education of Black youth has been Jawanza Kunjufu. In a number of important publications he has outlined an African-centred approach to the education of children and young people of African descent. He argues for an approach to education that rejects the Eurocentric ideals of this discipline, which has led to the pathologizing of the

African child – the assumption that there is something inherently wrong with these people.[95]

In a later book Kunjufu stresses the need for the education of Black youth to be rooted within African-centred concepts of living. He claims that these concepts are often at variance with Eurocentric perspectives and worldviews.[96]

The overarching ideas and concepts for Kunjufu's vision can be found in a later publication. In *Critical Issues in Educating African American Youth,* the author outlines the fundamental characteristics of his powerful argument in a question and answer format.[97] Kunjufu argues for a curriculum that recognizes the traditional ethos of community and mutuality that has underpinned African concepts of being and existence since the dawn of time. He asserts that this ethos has had a profound influence upon Judaeo-Christian traditions that have governed a great deal of human philosophical thought in the West for the previous two millennia.[98]

It can be argued that the most important of Kunjufu's contributions to the debate on the education of African youth has been in the contentious area of educating Black males. In a highly influential series of books, Kunjufu outlines the endemic role of racism within Eurocentric visions of education which have exerted a profoundly negative effect upon Black boys. The racism inherent within these systems has led to the mass underachievement and alienation of Black boys in the educational system in the United States of America.[99] He believes that one of the factors which contribute to the poor performance of Black boys in school is the often unconscious racist perceptions of White teachers. White teachers identify these growing young men as physical threats.[100]

Issues and concerns arising from the British context

Jawanza Kunjufu's specialized work with Black boys has influenced and encouraged a number of researchers in Britain to look at the state education system and its impact upon the schooling of African-Caribbean boys. Reva Klein outlines the work of *Kwesi,* a mentoring[101] programme for African-Caribbean boys in Birmingham that attempts to address issues of disaffection and exclusion in primary and secondary schools in that city,[102] emphasizing its positive attempts to provide Black boys with suitable role models from which they can gain a positive notion of Black masculinity.

Similarly, Gloria Morgan in her work with disaffected Black children acknowledges the importance of Kunjufu. She highlights the roles played by poor teaching, peer pressure and the lack of positive role models in the poor performance of Black males in state schools in Britain.[103] Mike Vance argues that effective teaching strategies for African-Caribbean children in British state schools need to be conscious of, and should affirm, particular elements of Black cultural life. These cultural factors include the facility of 'call and response' (the ongoing dialogue between an individual leading a *performance* and the audience) and the cultural related concepts of storytelling.[104]

In the British context not all educational practitioners and theorists agree with Kunjufu's seemingly dogmatic, African-centred approaches to education. Tony Sewell, for example, argues that a seemingly simplistic recourse to an African-centred approach is neither helpful nor wholly desirable for the British context. He insists that appropriate schooling for Black males needs to engage with issues of power and resistance. Educational approaches must look beyond the stereotypical conventions of 'race', lack of male role models and the neo-conservative doctrines of Afrocentricity or African-centred doctrines.[105]

David Gillborn[106] and Mairtin Mac an Ghaill,[107] in their respective studies in state secondary schools, have highlighted the experiences of Black pupils. Both authors provide a tentative thesis towards a more positive vision of schooling for these children.

Jim Cummins gives an overview of the means by which minority ethnic pupils have been excluded from the central debates in the development and planning of subject-content teaching in schools in the United Kingdom. From his research, he observed that the teaching strategies in state schools tended to be either 'naïvely assimilatory or . . . seen as culturally neutral.'[108] Cummins pleads for an educational process that acknowledges and builds upon the prior experience and learning of minority ethnic pupils. This approach is one that offers opportunities for greater engagement with the teaching and learning process for children from ethnic backgrounds, who are not members of the dominant 'host' community.

Supplementary schooling

The continued failures of the state education system to meet the needs of African-Caribbean children has led to the growth of an alternative arena in which the education of Black children has been undertaken. The seminal work of Edward Coard gave expression to the, hitherto, anecdotal frustrations that have been articulated by many parents and guardians of Black children in Britain.[109] Many Black parents had long felt that the British educational system was failing African-Caribbean children. One of the chief products of this continual failure has been the development of the supplementary school. George S. Richards defines the supplementary school thus: 'Supplementary education may be defined as a system of schooling which is provided outside, and in addition to, mainstream state education.'[110]

Richards outlines the development of supplementary schools which have been instrumental in providing a communitarian ethic that attempts to offer assistance with curriculum subjects found in state schools. Supplementary schools often incorporate an African-centred approach to the teaching and learning process in order to promote self-esteem and emotional growth.[111] The importance of supplementary schools is also discussed by Corinne Julius who reports on one such community venture in Brixton. Julius cites the work of Heidi Safia Mirza, an academic who has made important studies on the issue of supplementary education. The latter writes:

> British State schooling, despite a recent history of multicultural initiatives, still operates with predominantly taken-for-granted assumptions of Whiteness as normative. Black supplementary schools provide a space to challenge such assumptions.[112]

Julius highlights the positive benefits accrued by Black children from supplementary schools, where Black cultures, traditions and history are the norm. Reva Klein believes that many of the principles found in supplementary schools are beginning to emerge within the state education system in Britain. Klein describes the eclectic nature of the curriculum in a large secondary school in Sheffield that incorporates African-Caribbean cultural norms and traditions.[113]

Within the ongoing discussion of the education of Black and minority ethnic children, questions of attainment and expectations are never far from the surface. Klein propounds the belief that when teachers have greater expectations and belief in the Black pupils in their care, and are able to communicate this commitment, the attainment levels of such individuals [will] rise as a corollary.[114]

In a later piece, Klein questions whether the findings of the Swann report of 1985, which highlighted issues relating to the education of minority ethnic children, have been understood fully and implemented. Klein perceives that teachers still seem to possess pathologized ideas (ones that assume there is something wrong with Black people) in relation to the Black child, and this manifests itself in predicted notions of underachievement.[115] Klein believes that the British state education system is continuing to fail African-Caribbean boys.[116]

Black underachievement and poor attainment are not inevitable, argues Rasekoala. There needs to be a concerted effort to raise the collective vision beyond the horizon of myth and ignorance.[117]

Review of curriculum materials for a Black Christian education of liberation

Specific teaching and learning schemes for increasing understanding and faith of the individual lie at the heart of most Christian education enterprises. Prior to creating this practical theological curriculum, I investigated a number of existing teaching and learning schemes, which had the expressed aim of attempting to teach and nurture young people of African descent in the Christian faith.

'Drinking from our own Wells'

One of the most important Christian education events to have taken place in Britain was the international conference entitled 'Drinking from our own Wells', held in London on 15 and 16 March 1996. The conference brought together a number of Christian educators, parents and concerned persons, all of whom had an interest in finding more effective ways of teaching the Christian faith to Black people in Britain. The conference was something of a first, providing an opportunity to explore more fully what had hitherto been a much neglected area.[118] A number of themes were addressed, including the need for Black churches to develop a model of Christian education for the British context.

The failure of the conference, to my mind, lay in the inability (or refusal) of this event to acknowledge explicitly the central themes and concerns of Black Christian education to which reference has been made in this chapter. My concerns and criticisms are summarized in the following points.

• With a few notable exceptions, little credence was given to the significant historical and sociocultural differences between people of African descent and people of White European origins. It has been the failure to acknowledge these different experiences and realities which has led to the continual failure of existing, White-dominated, curricula to engage meaningfully with Black people in Britain.

• There was very little mention of Black theological thought and its associated concerns as the major content and framework for any effective Black liberationist approach to Christian education. There was little mention of the historical development of this prophetic discipline. There was no mention of the significant pioneers in this field of endeavour. If one were to be cynical, 'Drinking from our own Wells' gave me the impression of being a slick marketing event, as opposed to an open forum where major issues of importance as they relate to the development of a transformative approach to Black Christian education might be discussed.

• The event was inhibited and constrained by a conservative, 'colour blind' theology, which seemed at odds with the expressed intention of the conference. In short, there appeared to be a real tension between the expressed needs for a culturally specific curriculum for Black people and a 'colour blind' theology that wanted to assert a bland notion of sameness or homogeneity between all peoples. I have spoken about the inaccuracies and dangers of this 'colour blind' approach in one of the opening sections of the curriculum I created within this study.[119] The strictures of this particular type of theological perspective, perhaps, may have explained why the liberationist elements of Black theology were not invoked to any great extent during the course of the conference.

• As a corollary to the previous point, this approach to the Christian education of people of African descent was unable to utilize an African-centred interpretative framework (or hermeneutic) for reading and re-reading biblical texts. The model of Christian education which emerged throughout the course of the conference was one that failed to move beyond the merely superficial – the need for positive Black images in any teaching and learning scheme. Undoubtedly positive images are of immense importance, but to suggest that this is the extent to which specific reference should be made in any curriculum created for Black people is both simplistic and naïve. Gayraud Wilmore[120] and Albert Rabateau,[121] to name but two, assert that Black people during, and subsequent to, the era of slavery have possessed different ways of understanding the Bible and expressing their Christian faith. I believe the significance of their arguments extend beyond the merely visual.[122]

There are and remain significant differences in how people with varied experiences, histories and cultures will express and gain meaning from what it means to be a follower of Christ. It is this central fact which provides a crucial rationale for the necessity of a Black Christian education of liberation for Britain.

A reliance upon the idea that significant differences between British/European and African-centred approaches to Christianity can be expressed solely through the inclusion of pictures of people of colour, leads to the absurdity of tokenism. This form of tokenism is manifested in ludicrous and often insulting attempts at crude *colourization*. The colourization, of which I speak, is the belated attempt to insert pictures of Black or other people of colour into the text after the main body of the Christian education material has already been written. Consequently, there is little or no attempt to acknowledge a specific Black interpretative framework (herme-neutic) to the Bible or the experience of being a Christian. Most usually, a White, Eurocentric perspective will continue to be the dominant theme running through the curriculum.

'Drinking from our own Wells' concluded with the launch of *Echoes*, an import from the United States, which was promoted as the answer to the continuing dilemma of finding culturally appro-priate material with which to teach the Christian faith to Black people in Britain. One of the biggest companies producing Christ-ian education resources for African-American people in the United States of America is David C. Cook. The principal title in its resource catalogue that purports to be 'ethnically identifiable Sun-day School literature'[123] is *Echoes*.

Echoes

Echoes is an exhaustive Christian education curriculum written pri-marily for African-American young people. The wealth of material caters for children from kindergarten through to high school. There is much that is hugely impressive about *Echoes*. The various curriculum writers have used a variety of styles and teaching strate-gies. There are stories and positive images of Black historical and contemporary figures that are juxtaposed with attempts to link biblical narratives with African-American history.

However, there are a number of difficulties with this programme. My investigation of the texts reveals a pronounced conservative, evangelical approach inherent within *Echoes*. There is nothing wrong with this stance per se, but I am concerned that such an approach carries within it a normative, orthodox perspective that tends to support or even justify the status quo. This theological stance does not seek to engage with the historical experiences of Black people and their faith journeys within the many situations where White power and control is the norm. This failure to engage with historical roots of Black Christianity in the United States leads to a seemingly inevitable failure. That failure is the absence of any critical reflection and investigation into the means by which the Christian faith was used as an ideological tool in the oppression and negation of the African self by slave and post-colonial societies in the Americas, Africa and in Europe.

Echoes' shortcomings are exemplified in its lack of awareness of the subversive nature of Black Christian expression. Equally, there is little evidence of the liberation-inspired metanarratives (or big stories) of African-American people over the past five hundred years.

Umalusi

An alternative model for the Christian education of children of African descent can be found in a programme called *Umalusi*.[124] *Umalusi* emanates from the Republic of Southern Africa. Unlike *Echoes*, it is not overly conservative or didactic (instructional). As a result the theological reflections are less prescriptive. The material for young children through to early teens is dialogical in nature and invites children to engage actively with the teaching and learning process in a manner that is not clearly evident in *Echoes*. The material is conscious of the context in which it and the children are located, and attempts to reflect the realities of South Africa in the era of apartheid. (The material was written in the early 1980s.)

Given its awareness of the contextual issues that impact upon the lives of South African children there appears to be a glaring omission in the text. I have not found any ideological commitment to the empowerment or liberation of Black, African people. The text is surprisingly neutral and seems strangely divorced from the liberation struggles in that country.

Given the integral role the Christian churches played in the liberation struggle in Southern Africa this omission is most surprising. The programme has also failed to engage with or recognize the importance of developmental Black theology in South Africa, where the struggle for liberation was a broad coalition between people of different religious groups and the churches. This partnership was important, given the fact that some churches could not be used as centres of education for liberation as they were White controlled. Equally, I am struck by the lack of engagement with pre-colonial, traditional African religions. There has been a crucial syncretism between traditional religio-cultural African belief systems and the Christian faith.[125] This syncretism has given rise to hybrid, eclectic expressions of Christianity across the African diaspora. Given this phenomenon, the lack of awareness with regard to Christian education is an unfortunate oversight.

Fashion Me a People

One of the most important theorists and practitioners in the Christian education of people of African descent has been Joyce Bailey. She writes from a Caribbean context to describe the theological rationale which underpinned the process that gave rise to a newly developed Christian education programme within that cultural environment.[126] Bailey's insists on the need for the Caribbean church to come of age. This new found maturity will reject the colonial and dominant European ethic that has been all pervasive in the historical development of that part of the world.[127]

In the early 1980s, the Caribbean Conference of Churches produced an all-age Christian education curriculum entitled *Fashion Me a People*.[128] This teaching and learning scheme was influenced by the research of Joyce Bailey, who served as the Editor-in-Chief of the project. *Fashion Me a People* was the first contextual Christian education teaching and learning scheme for Caribbean people produced under the auspices of the Caribbean Conference of Churches – an overarching, ecumenical, Pan-Caribbean organisation.

The material in *Fashion Me a People* attempts to engage with the historical and contemporary struggles of the Caribbean. Attempts are made to analyse the many pressures that have been exerted upon the largely poor people of the many diverse islands of this region. The omissions in the text, however, are hugely important and have the effect of muting the radicalism of the whole teaching and learning scheme.

I was concerned to find that the theological reflections in the text as in *Umalusi* and *Echoes* do not assert a Black theological hermeneutic. The material also tends to be rather instructional. The attempts to promote a genuinely dialogical strategy of teaching appear all the more tokenistic when juxtaposed with the seemingly traditional, instructional approaches. While there is much to commend in the aforementioned texts, these materials would not facilitate the developmental tasks of this study.

Given the shortcomings of these existing texts, I accepted the responsibility of creating a different type of curriculum. *Growing into Hope* was the first Black Christian education teaching and learning scheme for Black young people in Britain. The theological and educational process that gave rise to *Growing into Hope* and some of the more significant outcomes that arose from its implementation will be discussed in the following chapters.

3

Bringing the Thing to Life: Creating
Growing into Hope

The reader may better understand the work outlined in this chapter
if he/she is familiar with or has access to copies of *Growing into
Hope*. These two books were written for Black children and young
people. They have been used, subsequently, with people of all ages.
In analysing the process that created them, I am speaking not only
to the needs of Black young people but of all marginalized and
oppressed peoples.

Central to the aim of creating a new model for the Christian education of Black youth, is the creation of an African-centred scheme
of teaching and learning. In this chapter I examine the creative
process that gave rise to *Growing into Hope*. I wish to demonstrate
how many of the central ideas of Black and Womanist theology,
coupled with transformative education, informed this practical
scheme for Christian education. I intend to show the relationship
and the creative tensions that exist between theory and practice.

In seeking to create this Black liberating Christian education
teaching and learning scheme, I was mindful of the associated difficulties of trying to convert theoretical concepts into models of good
practice. Within the literature relating to Black Christian education
there have been relatively few instances of academic study giving
rise to examples of practical schemes of teaching and learning.

In creating this curriculum I intended to combine the philosophical and ideological imperatives of Black and Womanist theology[1]
with the progressive notions of a liberating education. It was my hope
to create a relevant, practical theology for inner-city churches in
Britain. This enterprise was breaking new ground from the outset.

The creation of *Growing into Hope*: an example of a Black Christian education of liberation

Black theological reflection as the content of the two books

The task of creating this scheme for teaching and learning – *Growing into Hope* – began in the autumn of 1995 and covered a four-year period. Following the first pilot of material in the autumn of that year there emerged, over the following eighteen months, further Christian education material for major Christian festivals.[2]

In describing the creative process that gave rise to *Growing into Hope*, I have chosen to highlight the *Advent* (in Volume 1) and *Pentecost* (Volume 2) sections of the programme. These sections were the earliest attempts at turning Black theological thought and Christian educational theory into practical teaching and learning material. While *Growing into Hope* was developed in five sections, the theological and educational process by which these two books were created relates most closely to the *Advent* and *Pentecost* sections. The later parts of the programme reflect the process that was initially devised, and which is described at this point in the book.

The task began with my reading the seminal work of James Cone. Black theology has sought to use the Black experience as an antenna for listening to Scripture and testing the truth claims of White theological discourse. In doing so, it has provided an invaluable framework by which Black people might seek to understand, in a more informed manner, their existence and their experience. A better understanding of the world in which Black people live provides opportunities for a greater engagement with the necessary tools that can be used to achieve freedom.[3]

Using a Black interpretative framework

Black theology provided the chief resource for the content of the curriculum. It was only after I had read and studied the writings of Black theologians that I began to appreciate more fully their method of rereading biblical texts and reinterpreting them for a different context or setting: that is, looking at Biblical texts again in order that they might speak to a different time and location from the one in which they originally emerged. This process is done by reflecting on the text in a self-conscious way, in the light of Black experience. This process of rereading texts for a different setting (re-contextualization) was essential to the content and process of the curriculum and owed much to the pioneering work of the renowned African-American scholar, Cain Hope Felder. Felder, in an important article on this crucial process of interpretation writes, 'The implication is that, whatever one may wish to say about the Bible, there is a need for a disciplined scepticism regarding western appropriations.'[4]

This questioning approach to western methods of interpretation (a 'hermeneutic of suspicion') not only challenges and criticizes the norms and approaches of White Eurocentric scholars, but also asserts an alternative perspective that recognizes and affirms Black experience. Felder highlights particular texts that attest to the significance of Africa and people of African ancestry. The texts that he highlights illustrate the central place of Black people in the ongoing story of God's interaction with God's people. The psychological and emotional impact of this insight upon Black people, particularly Black youth, has been emphasized by Grant Shockley.[5]

The importance of Black biblical interpretation is highlighted to even greater effect by Felder and others in a 1991 publication that has greatly influenced a number of theologians and Christian educators on both sides of the Atlantic.[6] As I began to create the first section of the Christian education curriculum, I was mindful of the work of Thomas Hoyt Jnr, William H. Myers, Renita Weems, Randall Bailey and Cain Hope Felder, whose writings have given me some valuable insights for this book. These important contributions to biblical studies, and the advancement of Black methods of interpretation (or hermeneutics), have opened up the Bible for people of African descent. It was through the influence of these writers, amongst many others, that I gained the confidence to engage in Black theological reflection. This confidence is displayed in the opening reflections in each new section of *Growing into Hope*. These small theological pieces were, in effect, Black Biblical interpretation linked to the themes of Black experience and existence.

The writing of this curriculum was demonstrably influenced also by my exposure to the *African Heritage Study Bible*,[7] [in future designated by its initials AHSB] edited by Felder. The major portion of the Bible highlights themes and concepts that resonate with African cultures and experience as they arise within the Hebrew and Greek texts. When writing the early sections of Advent Week 3 on the theme of *Heroes*, I decided to focus on the figure of John the Baptist.[8] The AHSB describes John the Baptist as 'an Afro-Asiatic or Edenic wilderness prophet'.[9]

Identification of John the Baptist as an Afro-Asiatic man led me to use further material from the AHSB to develop this theme on *Heroes*. The section on *The Early Martyrdom of African Christians*[10] enabled me to create a link between this prototypical biblical character and more modern heroes of African descent.

I used the figures of John the Baptist and more contemporary Black heroes to describe clearly the principles and means by which Black people have been able to surmount the oppressive situations that have confronted them. The resulting learning and affirmation for Black youth is hopefully self-explanatory.

A Black Christian education of liberation and the Bible revisited

A number of these scholars have argued strongly for the need for Black people to engage with biblical texts. They emphasize the need for Black youth to enter into dialogue with Scripture in order that their own experiences can be validated. This dialogue can help such individuals to see the relevance of biblical material to the concrete realities of their lives.

One of the earliest proponents of this approach to Scripture was Jeffrey Stinehelfer. He outlined an approach to Christian education that could enable inner-city youth to see the relevance of the Bible. In an ingenious move he tried to relate the contemporary experiences of Black youth to the Bible. He encouraged Black young people to translate selected texts into a language with which they were familiar. The product of one such experiment is a fascinating piece of vernacular that could best be described as 'jive'.[11] Chapter 1 of John's Gospel is rewritten thus:

Dig this! The revealing of Jesus Christ!: God gave Christ the power to get his boys hip to what's happenin'. Then he rapped to an angel so that she could get the message across to his main man John, who clued everyone in on the truth of God.[12]

Stinehelfer impresses upon the reader the respect that the young people conferred upon the text, emphasizing the points on which the author of John's Gospel places particular stress. These young people clearly related to the text in a new and more engaging fashion, when they were allowed to infuse aspects of their cultural and linguistic experiences with what was formerly a remote and forbidding piece of Scripture.

A similar approach is adopted by Mc.Carey. He seeks to re-contextualize selected stories from the Hebrew Bible and the New Testament.[13] He attempts to re-enact well known narratives from the Hebrew and Greek sections of the Bible, transporting these texts into a modern setting by using the vernacular of Black urban America.

Exposure to these attempts empowered me to adopt a similar approach in *Growing into Hope*. In Volume 2 in the section on Pentecost, I scripted a short dramatic piece, rewriting the Pentecost narrative.[14] This sketch, entitled 'All Change', retells the Pentecost event in an alternative fashion using Jamaican Creole and elements of Black vernacular and speech patterns familiar to Black youth. The sketch sought to take seriously Earl Beckles' claim that Black speech patterns and dialects are not only vital components of Black identities, but also infer meaning, relatedness and affirmation.[15]

According to Massey and Denton 'Black English' is not a corrupt derivation of standard received English, but is an important idiom in its own right. Similarly, Carol Tomlin asserts that 'Black language' is an essential component in the identity formation and cultural practices of African peoples in the diaspora.[16] Consequently, the teaching and learning process needs to recognize ways of speaking if it is to engage successfully with children of African descent. Failure to incorporate these facets of African life leads to a loss of self-esteem and confidence amongst Black youth.[17]

Grant Shockley believes that self-esteem is vital to the development of Black youth. He argues that the practice of Christian education should be linked to the ongoing experience of Black people.[18] Shockley outlines the nature of this task in the following way:

> How to rationalize, conceptualize, strategize, and implement a Christian education program that has integrity and viability in relationship to both the Christian faith and the Black experience; and how to work at this problem among predominantly Black Churches in predominantly White denominations.[19]

Shockley highlights the inherent dynamism of Black church worship and details the means by which this force interacts with an experience to create the raw materials for liberation.[20]

The direct influence of Shockley's writings can be seen in *Growing into Hope* in the section written for the Sunday after Pentecost.[21] The theme for that Sunday is 'All Together'. In choosing this theme I wanted to highlight the importance of community, interdependence and the communitarian ethic amongst Black people. This corporate oneness, inspired by the Spirit of God, has enabled Black people of the African diaspora to surmount the oppressive situations that have confronted them. The writings of Shockley and others alerted me to the historical experiences of struggle, which found an antidote in corporate and collective response. These intercommunal responses have their origins in Africa.[22]

Joseph Crockett has undertaken some highly influential work that approaches the Bible from a Black perspective.[23] Crockett attempts to highlight themes within Scripture that reflect the African-American experience since the era of slavery. He presents us with a number of examples of how Christian educators can first interpret Scripture and then devise teaching strategies to help people of African descent learn effectively.

When attempting to write the second week's material in the *Advent* section,[24] I was influenced greatly by Crockett's approach. He links the experience of 'Exile' of the African-American community with Psalm 137, which is seen as a primary example for the exile of the African diaspora.[25] His identification with Psalm 137 led me to use this passage in the thematic material for creating a Black Christian education of liberation. I was conscious of the historic resonance of this passage within diasporan African communities – one need only to reflect upon the traditional Black spiritual 'By the Rivers of Babylon', taken directly from Psalm 137, to see the importance of this theme.[26]

Henry Mitchell suggests that the development of Black Christianity in North America, which began in the era of slavery, owed its development to a process of oral transmission, where the elements of faith were formed and nurtured through succeeding generations inheriting the story from the elders of the community. This process of oral transmission is similar to the oral transmission of Bible stories and their development.[27] I adapted his persuasive argument to create material that looked directly at the storytelling element within the lives of Black communities in the diaspora.[28] Influenced by Mitchell, I used the notion of intergenerational storytelling in the Black community to link Psalm 137 to the Black experience of 'exile' and migration.[29]

I was also influenced by Lawrence Jones. He argues that the notion of 'hope' is an indispensable component of human existence and occupies even greater significance within the life experiences and expectations of dispossessed, minority communities.[30] He contends that the notion of 'hope' within Black Christian communities possesses two essential dimensions: the here and now, and the promises of eternity. There is a struggle for truth between the nearness (or the immanence) and the otherness (or the transcendence) of God. Jones continues by stating that:

> The Black religious community has not had the luxury of dichotomizing faith and work, or religion and life, or the sacred and the secular. This is surely one beam of light it has to cast. The interface between time and eternity has always defined an area of tension in the Black religious community, the hopes of which have been directed to both.[31]

I used his ideas to develop the theme for the first Sunday's material in the Advent section.[32] His work provided the main title for the completed work when it was published. The overall theme for this curriculum is 'hope'. A hope grounded in the strivings of oppressed Black people in every part of the world. Jones reminds us that 'Hope must take into account the realities of historical existence . . . At root hope is not only a gift of grace, but a product of experience.'[33]

Developing the teaching strategy of the two books

I adopted a thematic approach because of my knowledge of, and commitment to, Black theology. In addition to the need to pay attention to this area, it was necessary to create a progressive teaching strategy that would bring this curriculum to life. Experience had shown me that worthy, self-righteous, models of teaching which lend themselves to satisfying adults tend to have a nullifying effect upon the younger people for whom such schemes are created.

This programme needed to possess a teaching strategy that would entice and attract Black youth to want to learn and develop. This approach would not make assumptions regarding the complicity of such individuals in the teaching and learning process. Rather, it would challenge, inspire and excite Black youth into a dialogical process, i.e., one where the teacher and learner share in the educational act.

The influence of Paulo Freire

Freire gave me a rationale and a method for creating appropriate strategies for teaching marginalized and disaffected Black youth. Freire argued that for oppressed people to be free, they must first recognize the condition in which they find themselves. One of the primary ways in which the oppressor controls the actions of the oppressed is by restricting the thinking of the oppressed. The oppressed view the world and perceive reality in terms that are determined solely by the oppressor. This constricted world-view prevents the oppressed from claiming their freedom.[34] Freire asserts that the oppressed need to recognize the situation in which they find themselves before liberation can become a reality. This process of coming to an informed knowledge of one's condition, and the accompanying process of developing the necessary tools for liberation, has been termed by Freire as 'conscientization'.[35] For him the oppressed need to come to an understanding that they are 'hosts' of the oppressor if they wish to develop a liberating education. Freire writes of this struggle:

> The central problem is this: How can the oppressed, or divided, unauthentic beings, participate in developing the pedagogy of liberation? Only as they discover themselves to be 'hosts' of the oppressor can they contribute to the midwifery of their liberation pedagogy.[36]

The force of Freire's writings had a profound influence upon the philosophy of education that underpins the teaching strategy of *Growing into Hope*. A teaching strategy that enables Black youth to be conscious of the history that gave rise to the circumstances in which they find themselves every day. Informed by this critical theory, I decided that the curriculum should adopt an approach which places historical analysis alongside contemporary situations.

When I wrote the material for 'Obedience and Responsibility', for the fourth week in Advent, I felt it important that the historical was placed alongside the contemporary. The intention was to provide Black youth with an opportunity to learn important details about their history and to establish links between that past and their present experience.

Freire asserts that liberationist education for the oppressed should be achieved in solidarity with the oppressed. There is no room for hierarchical and patrician models of education because these models reinforce the imbalances of power between the oppressor and the oppressed.[37] In *Pedagogy of the Oppressed* and his later works, Freire disparages the notion of a hierarchical, top-down model of education, where the learner is viewed as a passive object in the teaching-learning process. He described these paternalistic notions of education as 'banking models'.[38] Commenting on these instructional models of education, Freire writes 'In these banking concepts of education, knowledge is a gift bestowed by those who consider themselves knowledgeable upon those whom they consider to know nothing.'[39]

In a later work he suggests that dialogue is central to the educational process.[40] He argues that the process of education cannot be neutral. Education is an ideological enterprise. It either legitimizes the power of the status quo, or alternatively, becomes an essential component in the liberation of the oppressed. If the latter assertion is taken seriously and we are concerned with liberating people then education must become the path to, and the practice of, freedom. In detailing the adult literacy campaign with the poor and repressed peoples of Recife in Brazil, Freire highlights the raw materials of his teaching strategy for engaging with and alongside a marginalized and dispossessed community. Central to his strategy is the necessity to develop reciprocity between the educator and the educatee. The latter is not devoid of power or autonomy. They are offered opportunities to rename their world and to be participants in the shaping and development of new knowledge.[41]

Transformative education

In a more recent publication Freire, in partnership with Ira Shor, reflects upon this teaching and learning process. The authors proceed to highlight the major themes and issues in what they term 'transformative education'. Shor writes:

> Critical education has to integrate the students and the teachers into a mutual creation and re-creation of knowledge . . . The worst thing is to be in classrooms where students are silent or where they speak and write a phony, defensive language they invent for teachers and other authorities.[42]

Freire and Shor develop further their notion of transformative education. They say that this form of teaching possesses the power to change the relationship between the self, external knowledge and the wider society. This relationship, in which there is a struggle for truth, has the potential not only to transform the classroom and the resulting practice of the teacher, but also contains the seeds for a wider transformation.[43]

This emphasis on dialogue, not only as fine theoretical concept, but also as a principle in the practice of teaching, has been echoed in the writings of other educationalists and social theorists. James Banks provides a number of examples of how transformative teaching can enliven history and enable Black and minority ethnic students to reclaim their history. This type of teaching also enables them to see their historical roots and cultural experiences as being the norm and not some marginal distanced reality.[44]

Banks argues that this kind of education enables Black students to become critically aware of how knowledge is constructed, and shows up the ways in which the voices of the marginalized and the oppressed are silenced. Banks shows how the re-enaction of the events of the Montgomery Bus Boycott can provide the basis for a transforming dialogue. In this example, Black students are exposed to a process of re-evaluation that leads ultimately to the development of new knowledge and a growing critical self-awareness.[45]

The example that Banks provides is instructive, for it relates directly to specific points in *Growing into Hope*. In this programme, Black youth are exposed to historical events and are presented with opportunities to engage in a dialogue which helps them to reshape their reality. In the section on Pentecost, the material relating to the second week (written for the oldest group) refers to the work of Harriet Tubman and Rosa Parks. Events from recent American history are placed alongside the contemporary struggles in the collective and corporate experiences of African-Caribbean people living in Britain.[46]

Banks' assertions find accord with bell hooks,[47] who argues that this approach to teaching can liberate the thinking and the voices of women. This process gives rise to distinctive forms of knowledge and a reshaping of reality that is neither conditioned nor silenced by the normative power of patriarchy.[48] Mindful of the charge of patriarchy and the male-dominated perspective that pervades a good deal of the content of most Christian education material, I felt it important that positive images of women are included as core elements in the curriculum.[49]

Various sections of the programme are based on the assumption that dialogue is essential for effective teaching. In the first instance, dialogue operates as a specific teaching strategy. This approach invites adult leaders to use dialogue in their ongoing work. Secondly, dialogue is introduced at different points in the curriculum materials, through dramatic readings and sketches. These interactive forms of education provide Black youth with opportunities to become actors in both the figurative and the literal sense within the teaching and learning process.[50]

The influence of Hope and Timmel

In their work, which ranges widely across Southern Africa, Hope and Timmel use Freire's ideas to develop workable models that could help raise the critical awareness and knowledge of disempowered African people.[51] They echo Freire's assertion that education is an ideological enterprise in which the oppressed and the oppressor are engaged in a struggle for truth concerned with vital issues such as self-definition and freedom.[52] Hope and Timmel write, 'Development, liberation and transformation are all aspects of the same process. It is not a marginal activity. It is the core of all creative human living.'[53] They emphasize that liberation and transformation are core elements of the educational enterprise:

> Education is either designed to maintain the existing situation, imposing on the people values and the culture of the dominant class (i.e. domesticating people, as one tames an animal to obey its master's will) or education is designed to liberate people, helping them to become critical, creative, free, active and responsible members of society.[54]

The teaching strategy employed in Hope and Timmel, like my own, was influenced profoundly by Freire's concept of praxis. Freire saw 'praxis' as that action upon which reflection must be based if we wish to discover the truth that sets people free. He argues that true liberation cannot be achieved without the existence of a genuine reciprocity between reflection and action.[55]

Using Freire's ideas, Hope and Timmel make the crucial transition from mere theorizing to concrete relevance and application. This is achieved through the creation of a series of practical models of liberating and transforming education that are located firmly in a particular setting. The authors provide us with a fascinating model for shared dialogue within the teaching and learning process. They begin by identifying a number of themes and issues that touch the lives of African people. Hope and Timmel then proceed to develop a series of reflective and action-based exercises and games that attempt to elicit critical responses from the principal players in this educational setting.[56]

While this problem-solving and awareness-raising method owes much to Freire, it is not merely a restating of Freire's principles. By converting the central tenets of Paulo Freire's philosophy into a practical teaching strategy for change, Hope and Timmel move beyond the realms of theory into the real world.

My attempt to devise a curriculum that uses Freire's ideas in a practical, workable manner presented me with a challenge. Unlike Hope and Timmel's work, mine had the additional challenge of working with children, some as young as five.

Moving beyond Freire: Black theology meets transformative education

A number of writers, particularly Grant Shockley, reminded me that Christian education should be regarded as a theological discipline and not purely a social scientific one. Shockley argues that if one wishes to develop a liberating model of Christian education for Black people one needs to go beyond Paulo Freire.[57] Shockley outlines a five-stage programme for such a liberating model. This model uses not only educational theory, but clearly engages with Black theological ideas. It assumes that the God of love is involved in the struggles of oppressed and marginalized peoples. This emphasis is not explicit in a great deal of Freire's work. While Freire's work has provided an excellent ideological teaching strategy for the task of educating marginalized and oppressed peoples, it lacks a coherent theological rationale. He hints at the work of God, but does not explore this in an overt fashion. In many respects, his work is very human-centred, with little or no conception of the transcendent nature of God manifested in the Holy Spirit, and God's continued involvement with human kind.[58] Cheryl Bridges

Johns has critiqued Freire's lack of explicit God-centred thinking, and has sought to offer a theological rationale that is missing from his work.[59]

In his theological argument for a programme of Black Christian education, Shockley states that:

> The center of education for liberation occurs when persons are able to utilize their capacities of self-transcendence to evaluate reality, and as subjects, of naming the world instead of being named by it.[60]

This point is crucial. It inspired me to see why self-definition is an essential core component of the practical curriculum I sought to devise. There are a number of occasions in which this expressed intent is manifested within *Growing into Hope*. The most explicit example can be found in the section on Advent Week 1, in the material for the oldest group.[61]

I wanted to find a practical way of dealing with issues of self-definition. I tried to achieve this through an exercise that portrays graphically how oppressed and marginalized people have their world defined for them. The exercise involves Black young people taking on the role of objects.

Shockley's vision for Christian education finds its source in Black theology. He shares Black theology's view that God is predisposed towards poor and marginalized people.[62] This thinking led me to use Black theology to highlight the liberating impulse of the gospel.[63] Shockley argues that appropriate Christian education for people of African descent should be anchored to the realities of their experience.

The influence of liberation theology

Liberation theology, particularly the work of Schipani, was very important for my work.[64] Schipani, drawing on the work of Gutierrez,[65] seeks to bring together the main ideas of liberation theology and the educational process. He associates his strategy of teaching and learning, in which there is a struggle for truth (that is inherent within liberation theology), with the Bible.[66]

Schipani argues that liberation theology guides the search for relevance and ownership in this process of Christian education for oppressed and marginalized peoples. He reminds us that a key idea in liberation theology is that the Kingdom of God is in essence a subversion of the traditional values that govern a world dominated by global capitalism and White, western power and influence. He states that 'The divine Commonwealth is an upside down kingdom that calls for personal conversion and a comprehensive restructuring of the world.'[67]

This belief in a radical re-visioning and understanding of the world led me to develop the two consecutive weeks of material (for Pentecost), which focus upon change and community.[68] The first week highlights the individual change that is inspired by the Holy Spirit, as described in Acts 2. The following week looks at the development of an interpersonal, semi-socialist base community of faith. My reading of liberation theology in conjunction with Christian education inspired the creation of this material.

The influence of Schipani was supplemented by Frank Marangos, who argues that in liberation theology,

> The gospel, therefore, as the proclamation of authentic existence, is also a message of hope to individuals who are persistently denied such an authenticity by the present world order. Liberation theology places eschatological hope at the centre of Christian education.[69]

Marangos stresses that Christian education, when informed by the central ideas of liberation theology, possesses an ideological intent. This intent is one that is rightly suspicious of the common assumptions regarding the ills of the world, and envisages a new creation that is radically different from the one we know.

The works of Marangos, Schipani and Gutierrez owe a great deal to Freire and the concept of praxis, particularly as it relates to human development and the nurturing of critical thinking and understanding. Marangos contends that praxis should lie at the heart of the Christian educational enterprise, for authentic change cannot emerge without praxis – reflection and action.[70]

The influence of Thomas Groome and his notion of shared praxis

Thomas Groome has been a major proponent of an approach to Christian religious education that regards the praxis model as essential for the teaching and learning enterprise.[71] Groome, in a later work, develops further his notion of praxis into an overarching concept for Christian religious education.[72] In this seminal work, he outlines an approach he calls 'shared praxis', which he describes as being:

> A participative and dialogical pedagogy in which people reflect critically on their own historical agency in time and place and on their socio-cultural reality, have access together to Christian story/vision and personally appropriate it in community with the creative intent of renewed praxis in Christian faith towards God's reign for all creation.[73]

Groome details an approach that attempts to link the individual to a process of critical reflection and dialogue. These elements, in turn, are combined with the sacred stories (or narratives), in order that the Christian story/vision can be realized. This process culminates in the final phase of this approach. This final act is a search for the truth that enables participants to make the Christian story their own.[74] Groome argues that participants should be empowered to appropriate the story/vision in order that they can own it, and then remake it, so that they can be set free.

In order to support and empower the many children's and youth workers in this study, I created a number of training exercises and activities to assist these individuals to engage with and use the materials that would become *Growing into Hope*. These training exercises were created to enable adult leaders to understand and visualize some of the philosophical, psychological and socio-cultural issues involved in the Christian education of Black youth.

In the introductory material in Volume 2 of *Growing into Hope*, I developed an exercise entitled, 'Are We In the Story?'[75] This exercise is intended to help leaders understand more clearly a process that has afflicted African people for approximately five hundred years. A process of miseducation and biased, self-serving teaching strategies have led African people to develop a negative psychological condition manifested primarily as self-denial. This can be seen in the inability of colonized people to assert their own worth, or to see themselves reflected positively in popular stories, myths or historical events.

The aim of this training exercise is to describe clearly one of the principal sub-texts of *Growing into Hope*, namely, the need for oppressed people to use the story/vision for their ultimate liberation. This work enables Black youth (in fact all marginalized peoples) to claim the gospel of Jesus Christ as their own.

A crucial facet of Groome's teaching strategy is the notion of inculturation: the expression of the gospel through a specific culture (located in a specific period of time). This process includes appropriate re-setting of the sacred narrative, bringing the story to life and localizing the story/vision.[76] On this subject Groome writes:

> Christian faith is expressed in people's lives through symbols and modes native to their culture. It is a source of transformation for the cultural context – each cultural expression of it renews and enriches the universal Christian community.[77]

When I created the early sections of *Growing into Hope*, I was mindful of the need to inculturate aspects of the story/vision so that Black youth could psychologically and emotionally make the Christian gospel their own. Examples of this can be found in *Growing into Hope*, particularly in the section on Pentecost Sunday in the material for the middle and oldest groups.[78] The impact this material had upon Black youth will be detailed at a later point in this book.

The writing of *Growing into Hope*: a balance between idealism and pragmatism

Christian education programmes in many inner-city churches in Britain lack resources (both human and financial) and cater for decreasing numbers. A number of junior churches and Sunday schools in Britain are still wedded emotionally to the halcyon days of the past. This was a seemingly prosperous time when the numbers of children attending church were considerably higher than is presently the case, and the effectiveness of Christian education could be seen in the weekly 'conversions' to Christ.[79]

As one surveys the scene of junior church and Sunday school in many churches in Britain today, their halcyon days are clearly past. In attempting to create a curriculum that would have an impact upon the practice of Christian education amongst Black youth, I was mindful of the historical resonance of the past that has clouded the perceptions of generations of junior church and Sunday school leaders.[80]

In addition to this difficulty, there was the inherently conservative nature of many of the older African-Caribbean worshippers in the inner-city churches, where the material would be piloted. Many of these older people had migrated from the Caribbean in the mass movement of the 1950s and 1960s, having first being exposed to the full force of colonial miseducation. These older African-Caribbean people had received the biased, self-serving teachings of British imperialism, which asserted the superiority of European aesthetics and culture. The pigmentation of Black people was disparaged in favour of White, which was depicted as being synonymous with purity and 'civilization'.[81]

My knowledge of the social and cultural environment in which these older individuals had been nurtured persuaded me that a very radical and overtly political Christian education curriculum would alienate and frighten them. I could not afford to alienate this important group, since these individuals are the primary influences upon Black youth in their church attendance and development of faith.[82] Many of the Black young people who are the focus this study would not attend church were it not for the continued diligence and faithfulness of these ageing believers from the Caribbean. In short, the challenge that faced me, in the writing of *Growing into Hope*, lay between the two extremes of principle and pragmatism. The former represents the type of teaching and learning scheme that, as a principled position, refuses either to compromise or to acknowledge the inherent insecurities or weakness of the people (Black and

White) who will use it. The result of such a stance is often a low take-up of the material. The latter is indicative of a position, which, in its attempt to engage with the potential audience, jettisons all the basic principles and ideas that lie at the heart of what one might term 'best practice'. This approach may lead to high demand and subsequent usage, but little if any integrity exists within the text itself.

Growing into Hope needed to be principled and pragmatic. The pragmatism of which I have just spoken was juxtaposed with the need to remain faithful to the important sources that underpin this scheme of teaching and learning.

Another significant difficulty was the fact that the majority of the adult leaders who would be charged with the task of implementing *Growing into Hope* were White. My concerns regarding this group were somewhat similar to those stated previously, namely, that a radical teaching strategy might alienate or disempower the very group I was dependent upon to implement the material in these inner-city churches.

Growing into Hope does not purport to be the ideal model or example for the Christian education of Black young people or adults. The material was not written within a hermetically sealed, controlled environment. My knowledge of Black youth, and the insecurity and inhibitions of the adult leaders and the guardians who support these individuals in their Christian nurture, affected the writing of this experimental material.

Further reflections on the writing of Growing into Hope

In the first instance, Thomas Groome and his approach to Christian religious education influenced me. Shared praxis, as outlined by Groome, requires that faith communities develop generative themes. Groome defines 'generative themes' as being 'Some historical issue, question, value, belief, concept, event, situation . . . That is likely to draw participants into engagement.'[83]

The development of generative themes provided the overarching focus around which an appropriate teaching strategy could be constructed. My engagement with Black theology, and the substantive concerns that emerged from the writings of Black theologians, influenced my choice of suitable themes. My exposure to the concepts and themes of Black and Womanist theology gave rise to the titles that appear in the succeeding sections of the programme.[84] Some of the titles covered themes such as *Hope, Heroes, Wisdom* and *Change*.

The process of creating the programme involved the delicate exercise of synthesising the desirable with the possible. This process of aligning Black theology with Christian education[85] enabled me to turn theoretical ideas into practical teaching and learning materials.

Having developed the generative themes, there remained the final substantive task. How do I create a method that would engage and enthuse disaffected Black youth? The influence of Hope and Timmel was apparent in the method employed within the teaching and learning process of *Growing into Hope*. I tried through the exercises, games and activities to create a praxis (action and reflection) model of education where Black youths would be actively engaged in, and be full participants of, any teaching and learning situation. The rationale for this approach is explained in the introduction to Volume 1.[86]

An example of this process can be seen in the material for Advent (the third week of that festival), where the theme is *Heroes*. In the material I state that:

> The whole question of role models for black children and young people has been the subject of contemporary debate. Who are the appropriate people to become role models for young Black people?[87]

Clearly, one only needs to look at the many column inches in newspapers on the 'crisis' amongst Black youth to see the obvious relevance of this topic as an appropriate generative theme for a Black Christian education of liberation. In exercises such as 'Tough Face Tony' (based upon a series of moral dilemmas for a young Black boy),[88] and the 'Creating Your Very Own Black Hero',[89] I was linking ongoing concerns of Black people to the gospel of Jesus

Christ. The use of an appropriate generative theme brought the exercise to life and made the biblical and theological reflections (on the life of John the Baptist and modern-day prophets) relevant to the Black experience.

The influence of Jerome Berryman and his notion of 'Godly Play'

An important influence in the use of activity-based models of education for children was the work of Jerome Berryman. He describes an approach to the religious education of children, which he terms 'Godly Play'. He reminds us that games possess their own internal logic, and demand particular frameworks and rules in order to be effective.[90] Berryman's own work was influenced by Clark C. Abt, who commenting on the concept of a game writes, 'A game is an activity among two or more independent decision-makers seeking to achieve their objectives in some limiting context.'[91]

Berryman describes his 'Godly Play' approach as 'The playing of a game that can awaken us to new ways of seeing ourselves as human beings.'[92]

Berryman's approach to the religious education of children acknowledges that our way of knowing in intellectual terms, and the accompanying development, are important factors that influence the teaching strategy adopted by the educator to facilitate the child's learning. Influenced by Piaget's ideas, Berryman argues that young children in particular need symbols, images and other forms of concrete stimuli in their early stages of development. Berryman's comments lead us inexorably into the world of developmental psychology and the work of Piaget, Kohlberg and Erikson.[93] It is not my intention to rehearse the various complementary and opposing schemes of these differing authors. My own use of games to educate young people owes much to the thinking of these writers. An example of this influence can be seen in Volume 2 of *Growing into Hope*, in the section related to Pentecost written for very young children. In this section I attempted to use the idea of baking, and the transformation of an everyday object (namely dough) to explain what the Holy Spirit is and does.[94]

The initial implementation of the *Advent* and *Pentecost* sections

During the piloting of *Advent* and *Pentecost*, two dominant themes emerged, which were to have a profound effect upon the rest of my work. In the first set of observations, I noticed a distinct set of behavioural patterns in children of the 'Middle' age group.[95]

The attitude and behaviour of those in the 'Oldest' group[96] were relatively straightforward, in that they responded enthusiastically to the material. The opportunity to be actively engaged in the teaching and learning process was accepted with a good deal of enthusiasm. The fact that these sessions were led by White adults, who were not always familiar or comfortable with the material, served to heighten the sense of autonomy felt by many of these Black young people. In these situations, the sense of control of the session shifted from the White adult, who notionally held the reins of power, to the young person. The latter now possessed the ability to subvert the traditional teacher-learner relationship. As one White adult leader, called Sheila, said to me:

> Anthony, I wasn't really comfortable in that situation (when leading the session during the second week in Advent, when the theme was *Words And Stories*). I didn't know what many of the words meant, and I could tell that many of the young boys were having a laugh at my expense. But it was good for me to be exposed in that kind of situation. I didn't like it but it was good for me. It reminded me that there are times when I need to be prepared to learn from the children. I don't have all the answers.

This happened on at least two other occasions. This pointed to an early success for the process I had initiated. In enabling a group of young African-Caribbean males to be engaged in an interactive model of education as equal participants, the practice of Christian education in this setting had been changed, quite significantly, from the very outset.

The Black children in the 'Young' age group[97] were able to engage with this African-centred material in ways that were un-inhibited by issues such as lack of identity or low self-esteem. This apparent ability to engage with new teaching and learning situations can be explained, in part, by the findings of Clark and Clark.[98] Through their groundbreaking studies, these two researchers were able to show that Black children were conscious of differences in ethnicity by the age of three and four. A crucial facet of this appre-ciation of difference was the affirmation of self and an absence of any internalized preference for the 'other'. Clark and Clark, and later Wilson,[99] have shown that, at this early age, Black children have not internalized any negative perceptions of self. There exists through the early stages of socialization and nurture a positive sense of self and a high accompanying self-esteem.

Children in the next age group (the Middle group), however, struggled to relate to the material. During that first piloting period, I witnessed a number of children looking uneasy, embarrassed, unsettled and extremely nervous. They were uneasy because they were asked to participate and engage in a session that consciously identified with the development and history of their religious and cultural identity and heritage. Repeated attempts, by the mainly White leaders, drew increasingly embarrassed responses from a number of Black young people in this age group.

Having noted this, I decided to interview a number of these chil-dren. My interview with one child, a nine-year-old boy, proceeded as follows:

ANTHONY REDDIE (A):   Didn't you enjoy the session?
RICKY (R):   No.
A: Why was that then?
R: Because it was embarrassing.
A: Why was it embarrassing?
R: Because Miss [the White teacher leading the session] was trying to tell us stuff, and it was all silly.
A: Why was it silly?
R: Well . . . [Long pause while he thinks] . . . She was talking about things not being fair and stuff like that [from the 'Middle' material, for the First Sunday in Advent, on the

theme of *hope*[100]] and she was trying to get us to say some words, but it sounded silly.

A: Why did the words sounds silly? [Long pause. Supplementary question] . . . Do you know those words your teacher was trying to get you to say?

R: I know those words. My Nan uses them all the time.

A: Have you ever used those words?

R: Sometimes.

A: So why are they silly? What is silly about them?

R: Because we've never used them before in church. What was so special about now?

The final comment from Ricky was hugely significant. His reluctance to engage with the session was not due to unfamiliarity or estrangement, but to a sense of displacement. The words and phrases[101] that were used in the session were not ones he associated with being in church. During a group interview with half a dozen African-Caribbean girls and boys, between the ages of eight and ten, one nine-year-old girl (Rebecca) said:

We never do stuff like this in church. I felt stupid in Sunday school. That's what I do when I'm at home, not in Sunday school.

Another child in the group interview, Natasha (ten years old) said,

Why are they [the adult leaders] getting us to do this stuff?[102] We've never done anything like this before.

The behaviour of these young African-Caribbean people can be explained by reference to a phenomenon known as cultural dissonance.

Cultural dissonance

Cultural dissonance manifests itself in a wide variety of social settings. Cultural dissonance is felt when one feels out of place in a cultural setting that is different from one's own. For instance, a Black person feels at home where Black traditions, values, belief systems and practices are the norm, and feels cultural dissonance in the wider socio-political environment where White, Eurocentric norms hold sway.

Where the cultural dissonance is masked there is bound to be intellectual and emotional discord. People from minority cultural groups will find it more difficult. Yet they have to reconcile what they feel in their own cultural environment (that reflects their identity) with their feelings in the wider society (that is shaped by the majority culture).

The literature pertaining to the education of Black youth has many references to this cultural aspect. Language is particularly important for this discussion. Beckles looks at the link between language and dissonance that is evident in the experiences of children of African-Caribbean descent. These children appropriate particular dialects and vernacular, which are often viewed as the norm in the home, but may be ridiculed in the classroom by the schoolteacher.[103]

Similarly, Gillborn recounts the experiences of a young African-Caribbean woman studying at a sixth-form college. This young woman talks about the pain and anguish that she felt when she was subjected to ridicule by fellow class members for her use of Caribbean vernacular.[104]

The disparaging of African cultures, and their accompanying traditions and values, has led to Black people censoring themselves and to internalizing those things that give them their own sense of self.[105] In the face of systematic and systemic attack, which began in the era of slavery, Black people have either sought to hide and disguise those cultural components of identity, or have used these elements as a form of resistance to White power and influence. The latter can be seen in the use of language. While the African-Caribbean woman student was ridiculed for her use of Caribbean vernacular, on many other occasions this form of speech has been used as a way of concealing one's true motives or intentions. To put it crudely, if other people cannot understand you, then language becomes the ideal vehicle for subversive action![106]

My observations of the behavioural patterns of these children, confirmed at a later point in interviews, led me into a new way of thinking. The church environment appeared to be a forbidding one, and that is why these children felt unable to engage with this new teaching and learning scheme. In the earlier comments of Ricky and Natasha, reference was made to the fact that they (the children) were being asked to behave and respond in particular ways *in church*. The children believed that particular forms of cultural engagement were inappropriate for church activity. I pressed Natasha further and our conversation proceeded as follows:

N: We shouldn't be talking like that [the use of a Jamaican dialect known popularly as 'Patois']¹⁰⁷ in church.

A: And why is that?

N: Because it's not proper. You only do proper things inside a church.

As I have indicated previously, within the historic-mainline churches people of African descent are engaged in an ongoing struggle to express aspects of their identity and culture. This struggle continues within an overarching edifice of a White, European structure.

These Black young people were struggling with a cultural disso-nance that pervades the institution of the historic-mainline church. Hale-Benson is clear that cultural dissonance will have negative effects upon Black children, particularly when they are educated and nurtured into social arenas constructed with White middle-class children in mind.¹⁰⁸ Recourse to the important reports pub-lished on the Christian education and nurture of children in historic-mainline churches in Britain reveals little or no explicit acknowledgement of the differing needs of Black children.¹⁰⁹ The reports, although very professional and extremely helpful, work on the premise that one can make generalized comments and analysis of children per se. While there are many generic factors affecting children, the substance of this book, with its focus on the specialized concerns of Black youth, serves to highlight the shortcomings of these reports. Ironically, I would argue, that by focusing on a specific concern, in the first instance, this work is perhaps more generic than these national reports.

Initial outcomes of the piloting process: giving life to a Black
Christian education of liberation in the church

In the church that was to become the central location for the most
pronounced developments in the process that created a Black
Christian education of liberation, the Pentecost material was used as
the catalyst to develop an all-age worship service that included the
active presence and participation of Black youth. This service was to
take place in a Methodist church situated in the south-west part of
Birmingham. The majority of the members of this church (some 97
per cent) are of African-Caribbean descent. The children's and
youth work at this church was comprised entirely of African-
Caribbean youngsters, aside from a handful of individuals. The
service took place on Pentecost Sunday. With my support and
encouragement this church used the draft materials (from what was
to become *Growing into Hope*) as the basis for an African-centred,
all-age act of worship.

Crucially, this service highlighted the first major and significant
change in the practice of this inner-city church. A central feature of
this Christian service, alongside the active involvement of Black
young people, was the adoption of an African-centred, culturally
specific way of looking at the Bible (a Black hermeneutic) in the
context of worship. Black expressive cultures were also very much
in evidence in this act of worship. This service was to have an
important impact on my study.

Outline of the service

Stewards and minister enter the church
Call to Worship

Song	'O Let the power fall on me, my Lord' (Congregation)
1 Pentecost Liturgy	Taken from *Growing into Hope* (Vol. 2, p.117)
Hymn	'Spirit of the Living God' (Sung by the children)

'All Change'	Short introductory talk given by the minister, based on the theological reflections in *Growing into Hope* (Vol. 2, pp.115–16)
Hymn	'There's a Spirit in the Air' (Congregation)
Prayers	
A Dramatic Sketch	Based on Acts 2.1–13, taken from *Growing into Hope* (Vol. 2, pp.128–9). Performed by the young people
B Congregational Exercise	'Winning the National Lottery', Taken from *Growing into Hope* (Vol. 2, pp.132–3). Led by the children
Hymn	'When the Roll is Called up Yonder' (Congregation)
C Congregational Exercise	'Where's That?' (Part 1). Based on Acts 2.5–13, taken from *Growing into Hope* (Vol. 2, pp.133–4). Led by the children
Collection	
D Congregational Exercise	'Where's That?' (Part 2). Based on Acts 2.5–13, taken from *Growing into Hope* (Vol. 2, pp.133–4). Led by the children
Intercessory prayers	
Testimony	Congregation sharing how God has answered prayers
Hymn	'All Over the World the Spirit is Moving' (Congregation)
Benediction	

Brief reflections on the act of worship

At number one in the service outline, the words 'Pentecost Liturgy' refer to the liturgy in *Growing into Hope*. This was enacted as detailed in the text, with a child being given prominence in the liturgical act. At a further point in the outline, the 'Dramatic Sketch' (marked 'A'), 'Winning the National Lottery' (marked 'B'), 'Where's That?'(1) (marked 'C') and 'Where's That?'(2) (marked

'D') were all taken directly, or indirectly in the case of 'C' and 'D', from *Growing into Hope*. 'C' (Congregational exercise entitled 'Where's That?'(Part 1)) and 'D' (Congregational input entitled 'Where's That?' (Part 2)) were creative attempts to assist this over-whelmingly Black congregation (97 per cent) to gain a sense of the geography of the regions identified in the Acts narrative. Using the map in the material,[110] the minister invited a number of children to the front of the church. The minister encouraged the children to stand in certain places in order to denote the location of towns such as Pamphylia and Cappadocia. The genesis for this idea came from the material. (1), 'A', 'B', 'C' and 'D' show the means by which this new, African-centred approach to Christian education became a central theme within the worshipping life of an inner-city church.

In the marked sections there is an African-centred, biblically based interpretation (hermeneutic), which attempts to resonate with the past and present experiences of Black people. It signals also the desire for this form of worship to be inclusive, bringing Black youth into the very heart of the community of faith. Black youth are not only present, but also take a lead in specific sections marked on the order of service.

This service was the result of a number of important factors. My presence as author and researcher contributed to the raising of these issues and the resulting possibilities. The role of the junior church/ Sunday school leaders (three African-Caribbean women in their early thirties) was crucial in preparing and training the young people for their central role in the service. The role of the minister at this church was equally important. He legitimized and affirmed the creative developments that gave rise to this act of worship. The final component was the indispensable presence of Black youth and their willingness to become central players in this study.

Further reflections on Pentecost

The successful piloting of *Pentecost* gave rise to an important break-through in the creative process of developing new teaching and learning material. *Advent* had been a limited success, given the relatively low numbers of churches that had agreed to use the material. However, from the important advice and assistance of a number of workers with young people and the young people themselves, there emerged a systematic structure that would serve as the template for future writing.

In the first instance, the development of *Growing into Hope* owed much to the advice and assistance of a number of the workers with young people who provided me with invaluable information on the Pentecost material. In an early interview with an experienced children's worker called Dawn, I asked what she thought of the Pentecost material. Dawn is an African-Caribbean woman in her early thirties, who is training to be a primary school teacher. Our conversation went as follows:

ANTHONY (A):   How did you find working with the materials?

DAWN (D):   It was like a breath of fresh air – to have material that reflected the culture and traditions of Black children. With the pictures, stories and language, the children responded brilliantly.

A: How did you know that the children had enjoyed the material?

D: You could tell by the way they responded to the material. They were all enthusiastic and excited.

A: And that isn't normally the case?

D: No . . . Usually, they tend just to sit there looking very bored, or they play up for the whole time you have them.

A: What else makes you think that the children enjoyed the session?

D: The way the children were so happy during the session. The pictures in the book really fascinated them. They could tell by looking at the pictures that the people were Black people like them. When I read the story,[111] they enjoyed hearing it. I put on different accents and voices and they really got into the story. One boy asked me . . . 'Miss, I didn't know that you could speak like that (the use of Patois)'. I said 'Thanks a lot. I never knew that you saw me like that.' All the children laughed when I said that.

A: How did you feel when having to work with, and present, this type of material?

D: I was well into my stride. It was like I was liberated. I enjoyed telling them the story, speaking in Patois, using different voices, trying to make the story come alive. I had a great time. I was able to do things and show parts of me which the children or other people in the church probably haven't seen until now.

It is interesting to note the effect this programme of teaching and learning had upon Dawn. Her ability to identify with the material and to present it in an authentic and familiar fashion, I am sure, did much to enthuse and engage this group of young African-Caribbean children.

The role and importance of Black teachers

There are a number of references in the literature concerning the impact of Black teachers on Black children, particularly in Christian education. Janice Hale-Benson argues that the connection between teacher and pupil, where the two share a common ancestry and antecedents, is of vital importance in the educational process.[112]

In the specialist area of work with Black boys, Michael Ross in the USA has argued that African-American males are educated most effectively when the teaching role is undertaken by a Black male.[113] Ross asserts that the reciprocity and shared notions of Black masculinity and selfhood between Black males will assist young Black men in their education and development of self. In Britain, the work of *Kwesi*,[114] has been instrumental in supporting African-Caribbean males, by linking these individuals with adults who share their cultural background and heritage. While there are a number of commentators for whom the connection between Black teacher and Black pupil is a persuasive one,[115] academics such as Sewell[116] and Wright et al,[117] are more ambivalent on this issue, believing the teacher-pupil relationship to be one that is affected by issues such as class, nationality and geographical location. The role of Black teachers in the education of Black children is a complex one. There exists, however, within this study research data to suggest that the effective nurture of Black youth is best undertaken by an individual who has a shared cultural experience with the person in their charge.

Cultural dissonance revisited

The issue of cultural dissonance remained an important phenomenon within this study. Diana Slaughter recognized the negative influence of cultural dissonance in the lives of Black children, particularly when they are attempting to cross two or more cultural units. Slaughter argues that when one cultural unit is stronger or more influential than the other, Black children may be exposed to an element of discord and disjunction in their lives, as they move from one cultural context to the next.[118]

The difficulties in attempting to move between different cultural environments have been highlighted by Urie Bronfenbrenner. He argues that children are influenced in their development by environmental factors. He contends that behaviour is a joint function of the person in relationship with their environment.[119] He writes:

> The characteristics of the person at a given time in his or her life are a joint function of the characteristics of the person and the environment over the course of that person's life up to that time.[120]

The effects of cultural dissonance can be limited, states Janice Hale-Benson, if the educational programmes to which Black children are exposed are aware of the importance of Black expressive cultures.[121]

Having seen the pernicious nature of cultural dissonance, it was important that I devised a strategy by which this might be eradicated. Before I could attempt to tackle this issue head on, I decided to solicit the support of workers with young people, plus the ordained ministers of these inner-city churches in which I had chosen to work.

In order to share my initial thoughts and concerns with these individuals, I devised an action-based activity to enable the various participants to explore cultural dissonance through experience. The exercise I created was entitled 'Dancing At Home and Dancing Abroad'. The title of this exercise refers to a phrase often used by older relatives in my family to acknowledge the varying forms of behaviour that might be acceptable in different social settings, such as the home, or with White adults, particularly, in a church setting.[122]

In my introduction to this exercise (which was subsequently published in Volume 2 of *Growing into Hope*), I wrote the following words by way of explanation:

> When talking about *not feeling at home* I am not necessarily referring to the often recounted experiences of many Black people when they first came to these shores and were summarily rejected by the mainstream churches in this country. The sense of not feeling at home is far subtler in our current times . . . It is related more to the feeling that you are obliged to conceal your real self when in church and not display anything of your authentic cultures and traditions.[123]

Through my introduction of 'Dancing At Home and Dancing Abroad', I was able to alert many workers with young people and ministers to the importance of creating an informal and supportive environment in which Black young people could express aspects of their cultural heritage and identity. The following chapters detail attempts at consolidating this developmental switch from theory to continuing and confident practice. In short, could the tentative changes described at the end of this chapter, be consolidated and affirmed within the ongoing life of these inner-city historic-mainline churches?

4

Making it Work: Issues and Themes
that arose from the Piloting of
Growing into Hope

Creating the *Harvest* material: a specific example of a Black Christian education of liberation

When I commenced writing what would be the third section of material, I began by using the method I had developed when writing the two previous sections of *Growing into Hope*.[1]

In a number of the inner-city churches where this study was undertaken, I was surprised to witness harvest celebrations that were entirely Eurocentric in conception. There was barely any acknowledgement of the experiences, cultures and historical development of Black people of African descent. In one church, where the membership was over 95 per cent African-Caribbean, the harvest celebrations consisted of cold quiche, cucumber sandwiches and a barn dance! Without wishing to delve into the worst excesses of stereotyping and caricature, I can safely report that for the majority of Black people barn dances and cold quiche are not our thing. Despite the obvious dissatisfaction with this form of dissonance very little, if anything, had been done by the church to remedy this situation. Despite the fact that most of the congregation was Black, the church remained wedded to Eurocentric norms of expression. In order to help reverse this situation, I created the *Harvest* section of the curriculum.

*Developing a Black (African-Caribbean) theological perspective
on* Harvest

To create this section of *Growing into Hope* I had, in the first
instance, to locate an appropriate (generative) theme on which the
whole teaching and learning session could be based. The work of
Kortright Davis was to prove vital. Davis is a Caribbean theologian
who has written extensively on the developments in theology in the
Caribbean and North America.

Davis describes the Caribbean as a context where poverty is
endemic. Their economic poverty gave rise to political, cultural
and theological dependence,[2] with the result that the region was
hindered and undermined. Davis argues that the fight against
poverty and dependence can serve as a metaphor for the urgency to
develop theologies which use the context and the culture of the
region to address its concerns and realities. Davis calls for the
development of a theology that emerges from the cultures and life
experiences of the believers themselves, and is one in which the
sacred narratives of faith are made real in people's lives 'here and
now'.

Davis asserts that the Caribbean region needs to claim a holistic
view of an incarnate God whose presence can be identified in the
fabric of the natural habitat of these disparate islands.[3] Michael
Clarke, whose own work has been influenced by Davis, argues that
the island of Barbados, for example, needs to develop a sense of
indigenous pride that values the resources and folk traditions inherent within Bajan society.[4]

Reflecting on the work of Davis and Clarke, I began to 'play' with
a particular idea of God. This conception of the divine was based on
an understanding of God present in creation through the interdependence, mutuality and interconnectedness between God's
people in different parts of the world. In essence, God can be seen
in the links (or connectedness) between poor oppressed people
and their struggle for solidarity with each other, in the face of seemingly insuperable odds. In these struggles for survival and self-
determination, the many Caribbean islands have located God in the

midst of their everyday lives. In a part of the world that is racked with the pain of poverty, God has offered us a glimpse of the Kingdom, by allowing a tiny, seemingly insignificant part of the worldwide human family to assert its own visibility and importance. This is done by according these people a special place and space within the whole of God's creation.[5]

Converting this theological principle into the context of Black cultures and experience, with particular reference to harvest, we have to consider the importance of the foodstuffs that are produced in the Caribbean region. The Caribbean, although a tiny fragmented outpost of European colonialism and neo-American imperialism, nevertheless remains an important member of the worldwide (or diasporan) African family. A number of the most important and popular staple foods that adorn our supermarket shelves have their origin in, and have been created for our delectation by, the many peoples of the Caribbean region. The stone that the builder refused (Caribbean foods were once described as 'smelly' and 'vulgar' by a prominent TV chef), has now become a head cornerstone.

My reading of Davis, Clarke and Shorter[6] helped me to see the notion of an inculturated theology: a theology where the central ideas of God and God's activity amongst human kind are informed by the cultures and traditions inherent in the local landscape. These cultural and environmental features affect the awareness of individuals in their primary understanding of themselves in relation to God. God is known through God's own faithfulness in preserving and sustaining an oppressed and marginalized set of people in a specific place who, due to the cruel dictates of European colonialism, were never meant to survive. This belief came to me, with even greater force, as I remembered the words of my now deceased maternal uncle who commented:

Although Europeans meant for us to be poor, God has blessed us with sunshine and the natural things of the earth, so that we can survive. Anthony, you can't dead fi hungry (die of hunger) in Jamaica you know?

Influenced by these sources, I set about creating a series of Black theological reflections that asserted the interdependence of God's creation: the idea that even the smallest and most insignificant of people make an important contribution to life in what has now become a world village. This piece of writing was infused with the integrity of those individuals who are often deemed to be insignificant and invisible: the farmers and labourers who make up the majority of the workforce of the Caribbean.

The harvest material was influenced to a great extent by the work of A. Wade Boykin and his notion of psychological/behavioural verve.[7] Boykin argues that Black working-class children are nurtured and socialized in highly stimulating environments. These settings expose Black children to comparatively intense emotional and psychological stimuli. This, in turn, leads to higher levels of psychological/behavioural verve amongst Black children compared with their White middle-class counterparts.[8] In short, Black youth are infused with a dynamism and energy which, when utilized creatively, enables them to learn and develop new skills very quickly. One only has to witness the 'streetwise' intelligence of many inner-city Black youths to realize that Boykin is correct.

Boykin asserts that these settings have traditionally been viewed by White social scientists in pathological terms. He writes:

I believe we can begin to gain a better insight into noting the fact that social scientists have constantly described the home environments and immediate ecological environment of Black children as wild and chaotic. Why? Because when they go into the homes to make their observations, they find televisions on continuously. Stereos constantly blaring, a steady stream of people per living space and, of course, they conclude that these factors have deleterious effects.[9]

Boykin counters by claiming that these environments provide Black children with highly stimulating and relational ways of operating, which are rarely given any credence in state schools.[10]

Tony Sewell in his work with Black boys suggests that an emancipatory curriculum, one that is not based on an authoritarian, instructional approach, can have a positive impact upon disaffected subjects. This type of teaching and learning scheme attempts to harness the energy and improvisational abilities of Black boys.[11]

Mindful of these issues and concerns, I attempted to create a series of activities that would engage with Black cultures and experience. Concurrent with this aim was the need to develop a strategy of teaching that was influenced by the behavioural and psychological needs of Black youth.

The implementation of Harvest

A number of people who initially used this material claimed that the liturgy at the beginning of this section was the most striking and resonant piece of theologizing in the curriculum. In conversation with Doug, a minister at one of the churches that agreed to pilot the material, I solicited his thoughts on the harvest material. Doug was a White British male in his early forties. The church for which he has pastoral responsibility is a Baptist church in the south of the city. The membership is approximately 5 per cent White European and around 95 per cent African-Caribbean. Doug told me:

> I think in a context like this the harvest liturgy could feed into a communal memory. I suspect there would be some people where this might not have any depth . . . I think in some ways, in what you're trying to do is to get that resonance and feeling going for one's past. What I've picked from this fundamentally are those webs of connection that when we eat something or you look at something, what you're actually doing is looking at a great web of connection during which people are brought together. In that story about the banana,[12] in that chain, somebody carried it to market. Somebody bought it. Somebody packed it. Somebody shipped it, by plane or rail or whatever. And we take it for granted the great human labour that went into that whole operation.

Clearly, Doug had made the necessary connections surrounding the theme of the material and the nature of the interdependence of all human beings within God's creation. I will return to this conversation with Doug at a later point in this chapter.

Further insights from piloting the Harvest *section of* Growing into Hope

The faith community with whom the majority of my time was spent
was the Methodist church in the south-west of the city. This church
agreed to use the harvest material to change and improve its practice
in worship and learning. In planning meetings, the adult leaders in
the Sunday school/junior church, together with the minister and a
prominent local preacher,[13] committed the church to using this
African-centred means of working across the whole life of the faith
community.

The material was piloted at an all-age harvest service on a Sunday
morning. The service for harvest was not unlike the all-age worship
for Pentecost that was highlighted in the previous chapter. At the
very outset of the service, the liturgy was enacted, with four children (ages eight, ten, eleven and thirteen) accompanying two adults
in holding aloft the different elements and reading the prayers.

The adult coordinator of the Sunday school/junior church led a
group of twelve children in a number of songs that had been prepared specially for the service. The songs utilized reggae, soca and
other rhythmical cadences that are typical of Black musical traditions, both secular and religious. The musical input from the children was integrated with the whole act of worship. This ensured
that the inclusion of 'Black' elements was not tokenism or gimmick-
ridden entertainment which lessens the sacredness of worship.

The congregation was led by an African-Caribbean male who
read the story in the 'Young' section of the harvest material.[14] A
number of children were encouraged to participate in the dramatization of the story by carrying bananas around the church. The
pictures inserted into the text[15] were used to encourage the children
to engage with the theme in a manner that was consistent with and
appropriate for their level of intellectual development.

The children were supervised in their own space at the sides of
the worship sanctuary, working with pencil and crayon, colouring

in the pictures from the text. Simultaneously, the adults continued in their own appropriate forms of worship, chiefly through listening and engaging with the sermon, which built upon the themes outlined in the introduction to the harvest material.

This service was important, for it illustrated the means by which Black youth can be inculturated, that is nurtured and embedded into the household of faith. These children were encouraged to worship and learn in an intergenerational or all-age environment that resonated with the culture and folk traditions of Black people from the Caribbean. Ella P. Mitchell stresses that its is important for Black children to be exposed to the oral legacy of faith and experience by means of an intergenerational process of worship, communication and nurture. This process is a means of handing on the faith to succeeding generations.[16] Mitchell argues that the imperative for this form of action, and its effectiveness, can be borne out by recourse to the African experience of slavery and oppression.[17]

Charles Foster reminds us that children need to be nurtured within the whole community of faith, as they are the bearers of culture, both literally and symbolically.[18]

The following week, the children in this church went to the Sunday school/junior church, where the harvest theme was continued, using material from the 'Younger' and 'Young' sections of the teaching and learning scheme. Mary, an African-Caribbean woman in her mid-thirties, led the session. I sat in on this session, participating and observing Mary and the children in her charge. Mary had been the coordinator of the Sunday school/junior church for approximately eighteen months. Aside from having developed teaching skills through her studies, Mary was a gifted musician who composed and taught children songs that incorporated Black musical traditions and cultures.

The session I observed was lively, dialogical and echoed to rhythms of Black cultural experiences, focusing as it did upon harvest, and the food stuffs that are typical of African-Caribbean traditions. In the following week, I asked Mary what she thought about the all-age harvest festival of the first week and the session she had led the following Sunday. Our conversation went as follows:

ANTHONY (A):   How did you feel the service went?

MARY (M):   I thought it went really well.

A: What about the liturgy?

M: It was really good. The children who were asked to take part in that bit [the liturgy] really enjoyed it. They understood what was going on. Danielle said that she didn't know that grapefruits started from seeds and then became big things later on.

A: What pleased you the most about the service?

M: The enthusiasm of the children. They really enjoyed themselves. They love singing and taking part. It's just that we don't give them enough opportunities to do things like that. They all had a great time. There was no hassle. And, the younger ones, they really wanted to take a full part. I was really shocked at the way their parents wanted to get involved. That doesn't normally happen. The service kinda brings people together. I thought the whole thing might have been too much for them, but they handled it OK.

A: So what then would you say was the biggest difference, if any at all, between some of the stuff I've written and you've used, and what you have used in the past?

M: The material lets them do what they want to do, but also what I want to do. What you have to see, is that they enjoy doing it. Not forcing it on them, like how it was forced on me, when I was their age.

A: What do you think is the biggest difference between this new approach you are using now, and when you were in Sunday school?

M: There was all that attention. The children were on edge. They were not relaxed. I try to make things more relaxed. I want to give them [the children] a chance to express themselves. I try to meet them half way.

A: Do you get any feedback?

M: When I see them smiling and taking part and enjoying themselves, I know that I've done something right. I feel really good then.

In the conversation with Mary, I was interested in her sense that the children were able to express themselves in an authentic manner, when exposed to this approach to Christian education. This method of Christian education was interactive and located culturally within an African-centred framework. Mary felt that this approach enabled the children to display aspects of their identity that had previously been hidden or submerged. When I interviewed Mary several months later, and asked her about the relative merits of this approach, our conversation went as follows:

A: What's the best thing about this material, if there is a best thing?

M: I think the best thing, for me, was the amount of interest and the amount of feedback I got from the kids. If I didn't get that I wouldn't have felt sort of good in myself. But to know that they sort of understood, like I explained it to them yesterday [the previous Sunday], and they really took it in. From them asking me questions and stuff and I knew that they were interested. If they just sat there and didn't say anything or didn't respond, I would think that I hadn't taught them anything.

A: Do you think the children enjoyed being so active? Is that generally how you work with them?

M: Yeah, they do. They enjoy doing things like that.

A: So what do you think is the biggest difference now between how the group is, and how they were when you first started working with them?

M: The difference with this group is that there is more input. There is more input from them than there is from me and that's the way I like it. They are more settled and they actually listen to me. I don't have to shout or rave. They have just completely changed. Them having responsibilities and things. Especially when Brian [the minister at this Methodist church] does things in church and they do things in church, and that sort of helps as well. They have completely changed.

A: Do they like doing things in church?

M: They do, they really do.

A: What sort of things?

M: The readings, and simple things like collecting the collection. Doing the plays,[19] when they get a chance to. Singing. Anything that's, you know, where they are really involved in it. I know some of them might look shy, but you know, you leave them to it and they will surprise you.

My initial conversation with Mary was supplemented by a fascinating encounter with Evadne and Jelani. Evadne and Jelani were members of this Methodist church and had taken part in both the all-age harvest festival and the sessions led by Mary. At the time of our conversations, the two children were seven and six respectively. I began by asking them about the all-age harvest festival and what they had remembered and enjoyed about that act of worship. Jelani began by commenting upon his involvement in the opening part of the service, reading the prayers for the harvest liturgy.[20]

JELANI (J):   It was good when we read them stories, about God. And it was really good, because we took part and everybody did like the story.

ANTHONY (A):   So were you nervous when you were reading?

EVADNE (E):   A bit. But it was OK.

J: But everybody [loses train of thought] . . . It was a bit embarrassing. That's why I laughed.

A: So it was a bit embarrassing?

E: I liked when we was doing the thing, what's it called with those fruits and the labels?[21]

A: Oh, that one? The fruits and the labels! How was it?

E: Exciting.

A: Exciting? What was exciting about it?

E: What we had to do. And, it was nice.

J: I think what was good was the fruit and the display.

A: Hmmn. The fruit and the display, OK. Hmmn, tell me about the story your Dad read.[22]

E: Well! I forgot what it was about?

J: It was about God is good.

E: Was it? I can't remember.

A: OK. I'll give you a clue. Now you know he read a story about bananas?

E: Oh yeah. He was talking about the boy who had to carry it.

J: [Interrupting] Trevor [the lead character in the story].

E: On his head. And he had to walk far, far.

J: Into the market.

E: And he got to the market. And he stopped, 'cos he met one of his friends and he asked them if they thought, if they would help him take the bananas to market.

A: And did they help him?

E: [Shakes her head] And when he reached there he, hmmm, gave the bananas to the person whoever he was supposed to give the bananas to and then he went . . . Wait a minute. He had . . . He got his money for the bananas, he went to buy himself a drink, 'cos walking far and far and far and far, he was getting really tired.

J: Sweaty and hot.

E: Thirsty.

A: So, did you like the story?

E and J: [In unison] Yeah!

E: And I liked it when people read the stories they show you the pictures. If you don't know how to read, the pictures tells you something about what the story's gonna be about.

A: You did quite a bit in the service! You took the collection, didn't you?

E and J: [In unison] Yeah!

A: Have you done that before?

E: Yeah. Once before.

A: Once before. Right. Evadne. Have you read in church before?

E: Yeah, lots of times. Even though it was embarrassing, it's good to read in church and people to say nice things about you.

A: So people say nice things about you?

E: Yeah, 'cos you don't want to have a bad result.

A: No. That's true.

Clearly, the children at this Methodist church thrived upon the opportunities to be active and creative, not only in the Sunday school/junior church, but also within the wider arena of the worshipping community.

This latter point is crucial, for it highlights the importance of children being inculturated (socialized and nurtured) within the wider community of faith. Sunday worship is often perceived as an adult-orientated domain. There are countless examples of children being left out and being confined instead to overtly child-centred areas such as Sunday school/junior church. The affirmation and sense of belonging that is engendered when children are immersed fully within the whole community has long been a theme of Wester-hoff in a number of his writings.[23]

The developments within this church were pronounced, with all aspects of the faith community's life beginning to reflect the experience and faith expressions of Black people. This development finds support from such writers as C. D. Coleman, Bonita Pope Curry and James Tyms.[24] The effective Christian education of Black youth must take place within the wider framework of an inclusive, African-centred church. A community of faith, which reflects, affirms and promotes the Black religious experience and wider issues and concerns related to notions of self-esteem, identity and selfhood.

These developments in the worshipping life of this church represent important changes in other areas of church life. These changes represent the move from being a bastion of White British culture, to becoming a more African-centred community, which reflects the heritage, experiences and cultures of the 99 per cent African-Caribbean congregation.

The role of the minister in supporting and affirming a Black Christian education of liberation

The minister is a crucial component in the success of any church, in its attempts to create an inclusive and participative community where people of all ages are affirmed and offered the space to exercise and share their gifts. The role of the minister in shaping and envisioning a prophetic role that promotes liberation and transformation amongst people of faith is highlighted in the literature. Charles Foster has written extensively on this issue. Foster believes that the role of ministers is to be a prophetic voice, and to enable churches to experience the faith story in a form that sustains the corporate body. His or her role is to find and develop ways in which this story might be lived out amongst people of all ages within the church.[25] Foster continues by stating that the pastor's role requires a unique understanding of that community's culture and corporate experience. This understanding needs to be supplemented by the ability to read accurately those qualities that confer a sense of identity on that community. Foster explains this point by stating that to

> advocate the Christian vision, however, begins with the ability to 'read' the values, commitments and lifestyles of the congregation's culture in the light of the Christian story.[26]

In a later work, Foster argues that church leaders, particularly those who are ordained, must be supported and trained to move beyond the often-pressing needs of maintenance, management and administration. Administration and management should be supportive of and subordinate to a visionary, prophetic role that seeks to challenge and change the church. Central to this role is the church leader as educator.[27] Foster states that:

> The recovery of teaching is central to the survival of the faith community, moreover, in preparing persons to participate in, perpetuate, and renew corporate worship and mission which give the church its identity and task in the world.[28]

Allen J. Moore, as far back as 1969, stressed that pastors need to work collaboratively, empowering and supporting the laity so that the energy and the vision of the ordinary members in the pew can be harnessed.[29]

I observed and spoke to many ministers and to children and adults who experienced, at first hand, the work of these ministers. The work of the ordained minister within the churches in this study, according to my observations, can be divided into three broad types.

Typologies of White ministers in pastoral charge of Black-majority inner-city historic-mainline churches in this study

The first typology

This category is by far the most rare. These ministers decide that in order to effect the necessary change in their churches (in order that these faith community reflect more accurately the lived experience of its Black members), they must act in an overtly ideological and systemic way. These ministers inform the minority, powerful, White elite (who continue, in a number of cases, to dominate their church) that they should move aside graciously. Continued efforts are made to offer appropriate pastoral care and support for these individuals, assuring them of their continued importance to, and their ongoing role within, their churches. The focus, however, of the minister's attentions will be the marginalized and disaffected majority.

This change is intended to give Black members the opportunity to bring their expressions and experience of faith, and any accompanying abilities, into the central life of these churches. Explicit attempts are made to ensure that churches reflect the cultures and narratives of the majority Black congregations, whose presence sustains these communities. By its very nature, this strategy can be very costly for ministers. The three ministers in this study, who have taken this option, have seen their efforts met with opposition from the powerful, White minority members of the church.

Despite the cost, this is the most effective means of ensuring Black liberation in such churches. The Black members cannot be themselves until the necessary space is created for them to do so. The minister is best placed and has the necessary authority and the power to effect this change. A number of Black members have commented that unless or until the White minister 'makes a stand', they will not expose themselves to the insidious complaints of those wish to undermine them, in order to maintain the status quo. One can express this belief more bluntly by highlighting the comments of one elderly Black member who said:

See 'im dey? [referring to the minister of her church] If dat man get the house an' all the other things dat go with it, an' he noh want fi sey anything to dese people [a number of White members, whose actions and attitudes to the Black members are clearly indicative of a racist mindset], den why should a little old woman like me open fe mi mouth and say anything? No one a pay me to tek charge of de situation! Who dem t'ink me is? Fool?

In my interaction with White ministers in these churches, I have been at pains to stress that the decision to be on the side of the oppressed and marginalized is one they have to make for themselves. It is, by its very nature, a costly one. It is invariably the case that the very people one is attempting to cajole and encourage to move aside graciously, in order that others can be enabled to serve, are people who probably know the church rule-book better than the minister. These individuals can make life extremely difficult for the ordained person. At circuit, diocesan or provincial meetings, these people are often the powerful individuals who can engineer a situation, so that a minister is effectively sidelined or forced to move to another church. As I have often remarked, there are few more vicious people than 'good Christian folk', who are supposedly motivated purely by the love of Christ!

A minister's decision to act is not to be taken lightly. If ministers are going to act in these situations, they need to ensure that they have a good support group around them. It is vital that they alert other members of the clergy and lay staff of their intentions and actions. Mutual support and encouragement, bolstered by prayer and meditation, are essential if a minister is going to enter into the potentially threatening waters of intra-church politics.

Without wishing to sound trite or pietistic, we need to remind ourselves that, in Scripture, the price of justice and righteousness is often unpopularity and even persecution. The life of Christ demonstrates this most starkly. Conversely, Black members of inner-city churches do not need or require White crusading ministers with 'masochistic' or 'mock heroic' tendencies. For those who have struggled with long-term marginalization and disaffection, it is most unhelpful if in addition to these burdens they are saddled with the earnest, guilt-ridden conscience of some worthy 'do gooder'. It should not need repeating that one's actions should be motivated by a sense of service in the name of the Kingdom, and not by some implicit or explicit desire for congratulation and reward.

The second typology

This category includes those who operate in a more implicit and emollient vein, using the pastoral care model as their main instrument for change. There are a great many advantages to this model. Certainly, the minister who possesses the ability to be in solidarity with his/her predominantly majority Black congregation will be in a more advantageous position to encourage those individuals to use their innate talents and experiences in the church. This approach, however, although very helpful, does not address the central issue of power in the church. Many Black people are very sophisticated in their ability to differentiate between the 'minister who says he's on our side, and the ones who do something about it.' Or, to quote an older Black woman, 'I know that talk is cheap, and some of these ministers, all dem good for, is fe talk. Dem dey people never change anything.'

The minister has to take the lead. Black members will not make themselves vulnerable, when the one who is paid by the church and holds a great deal of influence and power is not prepared to make a stand. A number of ministers fall into this category.

The pastoral care model is most effective when it is used as part of a longer term process of empowerment and consciousness-raising amongst Black members of the church. The attempt to encourage Black people to reflect upon their stories of faith, and to view these experiences and the cultures as important resources for theological reflection, is best achieved through the supportive, affirming medium of pastoral care. Effective models of pastoral care that are culturally attuned to the life experiences of the faith community (in a personal and a corporate sense), remain important vehicles in the process of empowering Black people to be their true selves in the church. Sadly, even this seemingly non-ideological and pietistic model has been held captive by a mixture of bad practice and woeful ignorance.

All too often, in my conversations with Black people in inner-city historic-mainline churches, I have been disturbed at the number of individuals who have expressed disappointment that their ministers do not understand them. That in times of crises, often the last person they will go to is the minister.

The examples I have witnessed seem to indicate models of pastoral care that are purely Eurocentric in conception. The administrative machinery of the church has sent people with little or no knowledge of the life experiences, cultures or history of Black people, to churches were the greater majority of the members are of African descent. Given the distinctive stories of Black people, one might well speculate as to the means by which someone is going to care effectively for the spiritual, emotional and psychological needs of people about whom one knows next to nothing. The work of Wimberly and Lartey, for example, is offering us new insights into the complex issues and factors at play in the pastoral care of people of African descent.[30] If one is going to adopt the pastoral care model (despite its inherent flaws) as the basis for bringing about radical changes in Black majority inner-city churches, then that practice needs to be informed by Black theological thinking. This should be coupled with an understanding of Black cultures and the historical and contemporary experiences of people of African descent. I have attempted to address some of these issues in my previous publication, *Faith, Stories and the Experience of Black Elders*.[31] In this book, I outline an approach to initiating conversation with Black elders and between Black people of different generations.[32] I charge White professionals (whether ministers or social workers) not to expect Black people to disclose significant events from their experience without issues of trust and safe spaces being clearly addressed in their pastoral practice.[33] White ministers need to understand that in seeking to use the model of pastoral care there is inherent within this strategy a major limitation.

Within the literature there is an ongoing debate about the historical legacy of slavery and colonialism and the effects that this era has continued to have upon the selfhood of people of the African diaspora. An important factor in this debate is the question of accurate discourse. The physical, emotional and psychological struggles of Black people have affected both the alacrity and the openness of any conversation or discussion that is concerned with their individual and corporate experiences. Throughout the intervening centuries, the necessity to develop strategies of resistance in the face of racial oppression has led to elements of subterfuge and disguise in the behavioural patterns of Black people. Given the existence of such factors can one make any claim to veracity regarding the truth of Black experience and White authority? Hilary Beckles, commenting upon Black resistance in slave societies in Barbados, speaks of the strategies the slaves employed in their resistance. She argues that Black people survived:

> First, by taking underground those elements of culture which could survive without public display. These include aspects of religion and philosophic worldviews. Obeah, for example, survived underground in spite of legislation, which outlawed this practice as a social ritual or religious construct. Secondly, by openly assimilating European-derived elements of the Creole culture so as to achieve social and material betterment.[34]

Beckles highlights the essential disparity between the internalizing of Black selfhood and the façade presented towards White establishment and authority. It is this disparity that gives rise to the split nature of Black life: a duality that moves interchangeably between the Black internal experience of self-affirmation and the external experiences of negation.[35] Shockley asserts that this duality has been affirmed and sustained within a corporate Black religio-cultural life that is chiefly exemplified by the Black church. The Black church in the service of Black selfhood, argues Shockley, was the first institution that 'Supported their groping efforts to affirm their identities, worth, and aspirations as human beings and as children of God.'[36]

The separation of these emotional and psychological processes has given rise to a particular feature of Black life within White-majority dominated societies or institutions. That feature is the seemingly pervasive sense of cultural dissonance, to which reference was made in the previous chapter. In White-dominated societies and institutions, particularly in the face of White authority figures, Black people will conceal and disguise aspects of their existence or experiences. In short, there are some things they will not tell the minister. This is a major drawback for those ministers who adopt the pastoral model as their chief means of bringing about change.

The third typology

This category includes those ministers whose interests or gifts do not lie in the pastoral arena, but in the area of strategic planning, social action and project development. Given the often poor financial situation that confronts many inner-city churches, there has been a tendency to invite or send to inner-city churches, ministers who have expertise and experience in these areas. I do not think that this policy is necessarily wrong. In many instances, however, the majority of Black people in inner-city churches possess limited knowledge and skills in the areas of strategic planning, social action and project development. Often, in order for the church to survive financially, it requires a proactive minister who is not encumbered by the lack of experience and knowledge of the Black congregation. Ministers in this situation often implement plans and develop strategies without proper consultation with the majority of their Black church members. Unfortunately, this way of working, although necessary and a justified means of operating, can develop into a paternalistic and patronizing tendency that finds expression in *all areas* of minister–church relations. It is sad to report that many Black members voice with compassion, sadness and anger, their negative feelings about the attitude of many of the White ministers who have pastoral charge of their churches. As one woman (an African-Caribbean in her fifties) said, 'The problem with ****, is that he has a massa complex [a White slave master]. He acts like we're still pickney [children] and we don't have no sense.'

The majority of these ministers are well meaning. The ministers in this category are the ones who know relatively little about the Black people in their charge. Black people will most usually conceal

their negative experiences and feelings in the presence of White
authority. Some White ministers can use this to validate and legitimize their actions. One particular White minister said in defence of
his actions:

> But Anthony, I've asked *my people* [note the possessive use of
> language here!] if they are interested in doing Black theology or
> talking about Black issues, and they say no. They don't want
> that. They are happy with how things are at the moment. Colour
> doesn't matter to them.

In response to this statement, I retorted,

> Well, what did you expect them to say? Of course they're going
> say that. They are going say exactly what they think *you want to
> hear*. We've been doing that for centuries. I bet if I asked them
> that same question, they would give me a different answer.

On other occasions, I have observed Black members (predominantly older ones), express one view in what they consider a 'safe'
environment – when the minister is absent, and a directly opposite
view when the minister is present. An unsafe environment is one
that is formal, and White people, particularly authority figures
(especially the minister) are present. Alternatively, if people do
not change their comments, they are silent. Grown adults will be
rendered dumb and inarticulate. The corporate church and individual ministers have often viewed this silence to be acquiescence
and complicity. Often, this silence can mean dissatisfaction and
unease, but the context is not one in which individuals feel able to
express their deep-seated feelings.

Which minister is best – Black or White?

One of the important issues that needs to be addressed by church
structures and hierarchies in relation to churches that are over-
whelmingly Black is the question of who is the most appropriate

minister to serve in these contexts? In those institutions where Black cultures, experiences and expressions of faith are the norm (Black-majority Pentecostal churches, for example) this question usually has a natural answer, namely, that the ministers expected to serve in these settings will share the same cultural and ethnic background as the congregation. In these contexts, therefore, the issue becomes one of theology, personal disposition and ability. In terms of historic-mainline churches a whole host of more fundamental questions abound.

As I have tried to indicate in the first two chapters of this book, meaningful discussions relating to Black people in White-dominated and White-run institutions cannot take place without proper recognition of the complex issues of 'race', power and history. The presence of Black people in these churches speaks of a historical relationship between Black and White that is complex, contradictory and deeply problematic. The notion of 'the best man or woman for the job irrespective of . . .' fails to take into account the nature of symbolism, internalized racism amongst Black people and the historical legacy of White power. As such, this thinking is deeply flawed. Historical amnesia is not the solution for the challenges and opportunities presented by Black-majority historic-mainline churches.

Conversely, I have heard White ministers make a positive virtue of their ethnicity, by claiming that they can act as 'honest brokers' in diverse Black communities. These individuals cite the inter-communal jealousies and antagonisms between various African and Caribbean peoples, and within the diverse nations of the African continent itself. They are assured of the appropriateness of their presence in these churches by asserting that they are the ones who are 'neutral'. Aside from the casual patrician arrogance of this stance (it still smacks of 'massa knows best' and these piccaninnies cannot be trusted to run their own show), it once again deals in wholesale historical amnesia. This form of justification takes no account of the effective ways in which White institutional power developed a pernicious policy of 'divide and rule' – playing off different ethnic and communal groups against each other so that the status quo could be maintained.[37] If White ministers want to be 'honest brokers', then their role is to be agents of change, who will challenge Black people in their churches to be 'conscientized' (to become critically aware) so that they can understand the historic roots of some of their antipathies and rivalries. Those who exploit these situations for their own ends are the opponents of the kind of liberation they so often espouse, and their so-called commitment which they parade so proudly on their sleeve.

The solution to the question of which minister is to be found, in part, in Black clergy who are conscious of and informed by the historical and contemporary realities of being Black in a world where that very fact has led to racial oppression and marginalization. These Black individuals will possess a commitment to Black theological reflection and Black cultural expression within the life of the church. It is imperative that Black clergy are committed to collaborative styles of ministry in solidarity with lay people. The cause of Black liberation should be an important part of their understanding of the issues that affect Black-majority congregations. We need to reject the old rhetoric that assumed that *all* Black ministers regardless of commitment and disposition should be sent to Black-majority inner-city churches in Britain.

White ministers who are called to serve in these contexts need to realize that to be neutral or even-handed in some circumstances is to affirm the status quo. This leads to the maintaining of the existing oppressive structures, where a White remnant exercises a disproportionate and unhealthy amount of power within the church.

Prophetic, radical change: an example of a minister in the first typology

An example of a minister in the first category is Doug, the minister at the Baptist church to which reference has been made previously in this chapter. I asked Doug about his use of the harvest material and his perceptions of its impact upon his church. This conversation was followed by an exploration of the rationale and strategies he had employed to create a more inclusive, participative and liberating church.

ANTHONY (A): How did you go about trying to change the existing set-up in the church?

DOUG (D): We initially decided to have a word. We needed to challenge some of these White middle-class people who dominated the church and didn't even live in the area. Have you seen the church?

A: Yes.

D: Do you remember we've got a wall hanging? The Tree of Life.

A: Yes.

D: One of the things that happened was that in that wall hanging, where there is, I think, there are only six White faces. And for these people this became an issue. One of them, long after we had it, one of them came up to me and said to me, 'You realize that there are only six White faces in the wall hanging?' So I said, 'Well, sure, that's about par for the course. We are the ethnic minority in this church now' . . . But there is this mind-set, which is so imperialistic and culturally dominating. They refuse to acknowledge anything outside of their own experience, which they think is everything.

A: How have you managed to move the things on? To get the church to change?

D: For many years now, we've been trying to be a community church, not just a membership church. But there comes a point when you have to take a stand against the injustices you see happening all the time. All the White racists have moved on. We've managed to evict the troublemakers. They've moved and we're glad about that. It reaches a point when White people are not holding hands with Black people. It was time for those people to leave.

Doug explained how he initiated this process to change the character of the church by confronting those individuals who he felt were being overtly racist. Using the method outlined in Matthew's Gospel,[38] Doug proceeded to confront these individuals. He then solicited the support of church elders to assist him in breaking this impasse. The conversation continued as follows:

A: What led you to act the way you have done and take that course of action?

D: For me, this is all about justice and righteousness. We cannot take a soft option on racism. Not enough people will take the bull by the horns and say that this is not acceptable in the Christian community. Too often, the church is too tolerant. You have to be loving, compassionate and kind. You reach the point, however, where you have to decide what is acceptable. You can't just say to people 'change'. They need to be converted. It's a long-term thing. Like the dripping of water on a stone.

I concluded our discussion by asking Doug for an overview of his work and that of the church overall.

A: So tell me Doug, how would you sum up work at **** Baptist church and things in general?

D: I think what happens, or what has happened, is that, if you will, it is a bit like a river, going in a direction. It ultimately goes north or south, but there will be times when it meanders off and goes east a bit. And I think in some ways, ministry is a bit like that. I mean, there was a time when you were trying to achieve some change for something else. You're always going in some sort of ultimate direction or general direction, but it weaves about and meanders a bit. And we've been through quite a bit of a change over the past five years. Having been almost exclusively old and White working-class and first-generation West Indian immigrants, there is beginning to be a shift in that, and there are people who are going back to Jamaica and there are people who are dying. And we've reached the point where things are changing. We've started to pick up, I was about to say people in your generation. How old are you?

A: Thirty-two.

D: The likes of **** **** [he mentions an African-Caribbean woman in her thirties] have just joined the church. We've recently had baptisms of second-generation people. Mainly, professionals, teachers, social workers, probation officers and people like that.

Clearly, Doug is not a typical inner-city minister. Doug's actions and ministry are imbued with a commitment to racial justice and the creation of an inclusive church community that is built upon liberating principles. These principles are biblical. In attempting to be a catalyst for change, Doug acknowledges that harsh words may need to be spoken. It may be necessary that he become unpopular with certain elements within the church if justice and righteousness are to prevail.

Doug recognizes that the majority African-Caribbean membership requires a safe space in which they might feel encouraged to offer their talents and experiences within the church. It was necessary to confront the minority which prevented the creation of the much-needed secure environment. Doug's proactive engagement with the struggle for justice and liberation led him to side with the oppressed and the marginalized. This type of action, as Leyland reminds us, is part of a biblically inspired tradition that is espoused by Black Christian educators.[39]

Doug's approach to ministry is one that affirms the cultural heritage and experience of African-Caribbean people. His use of the teaching and learning materials was crucial to his attempt to reflect more accurately the culture and experiences of the majority Black congregation.

Doug's presence within this church, and his commitment to creating a liberating and inclusive ethos, echo the thoughts of Letty Russell. Russell advocates that effective Christian education, and the role of the pastor in that setting, should be a whole church activity.[40] She writes, 'The Pastor or associate pastor who views preaching and an adult Bible study class as his or her share in Religious Education has missed the whole point.'[41]

Outcomes from the piloting of the *Harvest* section of *Growing into Hope*

Through the piloting of the harvest material, the many workers with Black youth in these inner-city settings began to see the value of using this type of worship and learning material to liberate and transform the church. This process, which I have termed 'redefining the norm,' is facilitated and affirmed by the presence of a pro-active minister who is willing to act as guarantor of the liberating movements within the church.

'Redefining the norm'

In order to assist youth and children's workers, ministers, parents, plus the Black youngsters themselves, to understand the basic philosophy that underpins 'redefining the norm', I constructed the following exercise. Following the exercise, and the reflections that accompany it, are my comments on the importance of this process.

Doing the exercise

- For the following exercise, you will need to make two copies of a template (shown in Fig. 4.1). The template contains a story that is told in nine short paragraphs.

- When you have made the two copies of the template, cut along the vertical and horizontal lines, to make the sheet of paper into separate boxes.

- Split the group with whom you are working into two.

- In one corner of the room is Group A. They make up roughly 20 per cent of the total number. Tell these people that they are at the heart of the church; they represent what the church is all about; they are the leaders. All of them are intelligent, well-educated and very proud of being where they are

The days are short, but wait a moment, there is something on the horizon. Here comes the answer to all my questions. This is it!	The best thing about being your own boss, she thought to herself, is that I am not dependent upon other people. I can please myself.	Once upon a time, in a dark wood, there lived an old woodcutter. She lived all alone. She looked at the pictures in the air and thought to herself, 'This is good. I love all this. It is perfect.'
As the days became more and more difficult, the woman became increasingly anxious. What will happen to me? How will I cope?	There was nothing much to say. She looked at her reflection in the mirror and began to cry. She cried a big bucketful of tears. It was not fair.	The sense of peace and contentment, which had been a great part of the woman's life up to that point, was suddenly interrupted. The world looked completely different now!
Life is cruel, thought the woman. What bad things have I done to the world, or to other people, to deserve this? But the sky was silent.	In the morning, the sun was shining, and the woman went back to chopping wood. The birds were singing, and she thought, 'Maybe, just maybe!'	Childhood is a strange time, thought the woman. It is so very strange. It seems like such a long time ago. I can't believe that all those years have passed?

Fig. 4.1 Template for 'Redefining the norm'

– right at the heart. Being right at the heart is characterized by these people. *This group is given all nine squares.* (Remember to jumble up the squares, so they are in no particular order.) This group has to reassemble the story so that there is some form of progression from the beginning to the end. They also have to try and work out the meaning of the story.

- Then ask the second group, Group B, to collect their sheet. The members of Group B are not as important as Group A. *This group is given five of the nine squares. You can decide which squares you will omit.* Like Group A, Group B has to reassemble the story and figure out the meaning. They have an obvious handicap, in that they do not possess all the information.

- Give each group approximately fifteen minutes to try and accomplish the two tasks – reassembling the story and working out the meaning.

- After five minutes, inform Group B that they are not in possession of all the squares that make up the story. Consequently, they will have to try and invent their own bits to complete the story.

- When the permitted time has passed, bring both groups together. Ask Group A to retell the story. What do they think it is all about? What order does the story follow?

- How does Group A feel? Do they think they did well in the task?

- Ask Group B for their version of the story. What happened to them? How did they find the exercise? What was their biggest problem?

- Ask Group B if they think their story has any validity. Is it a worthwhile story? How does it compare to the story, as told by Group A?

Reflections on the exercise

The aforementioned exercise is a metaphor for the church and our corporate attempts to interpret the 'story' of the gospel. In the institutionalized church there is a central norm, which is based upon the experiences of a certain type of person (White, male, middle class, ordained, well established in the church for many years). These groups of people are right at the heart of the church, and are in full possession of the 'story'. They have all the parts of the 'story', and can attempt to reinterpret it in a manner that makes sense to them. They possess the greatest sense of belonging and ownership.

If you want to know who might be described as being part of that normative group, or whether you are a member of it, simply ask yourself these questions: Who are the people most likely to have their beliefs, wishes or perspectives reflected in the church? Whose personal inclinations, desires, expectations or particular understanding will be reflected? To put it bluntly, who can get their own way? By identifying the people, you will have defined the 'norm'.

Jesus is used to justify the norm

In theological terms, the norm finds substance and justification in the churches' identification with Jesus, as the central agent in God's purposes for a world in need of redemption. In much of our incarnational theology, we assert that the 'word became flesh' and came among us in human form. Jesus becomes the prototypical model on which Christian discipleship is based. Through the power of the Spirit, we are expected to conform to God's likeness in Christ, and follow Jesus' example.

Given the Christocentric nature of Black theology, it must seem strange that I am looking at the incarnation as a possible fault line in the creation and development of an exclusive norm that governs the church and often marginalizes others. If we look at the history of European art (iconography), particularly in its depiction of Jesus, we will notice the popularity of a White, very European figure – a figure which conforms to the growing ideas of White European supremacy.[42] By insisting that Jesus is White,[43] those with power have been able to link their own cultural practices and identity with the Christ figure, who becomes 'one of them'. In effect, a substantive theological truth is reversed, i.e., we create God in our image. The norms that are determined by the powerful are projected onto the figure of Jesus, who then justifies what the powerful assert as being true.

If this seems somewhat fanciful, then look at the procedures for candidating for the ordained ministry in any of the historic-mainline churches in Britain. Spiritual and faith values or qualities become synonymous with or are even exchanged for characteristics that equate with White professionalism and status.[44] Ordained ministers undoubtedly belong to Group A. The people who make up Group A in social and economic terms are almost exclusively White, middle class and professional, and are distinct from those they will lead (especially in inner-city churches), who constitute Group B. Subconsciously, Jesus becomes the model and justification for this skewed process. The Jesus who substantiates this process is the one who is declared Lord.[45] Jesus is Lord, and gives authority to his followers, who themselves become the interpreters of the story and are given authority to speak in his name.

In the interests of liberation and inclusion, greater emphasis upon the servanthood of Christ[46] would amend the tendency for those in Group A to take authority as normative, often to the exclusion of others. I cannot recall ever seeing a slogan on a noticeboard or poster stating that 'Jesus is Servant'. It does not look or sound impressive and, to be brutally honest, it does not make us feel good or important either! Robert Beckford's work constantly reminds us that the ministry of Jesus endorses the struggle for liberation of those in Group B, rather than the structural power and importance of the members of Group A.[47]

Whose story is valid?

Those in group B have only partial information. Consequently, they had the task of trying to construct their own story. It may have appeared like a thankless task. On the other hand, they were able to use their imaginations and ideas, in order to try and make sense of the story they were given. The task I am describing is not a new one. It can be argued that the peoples of the so-called 'Two-Thirds World' have undertaken the ingenious step of constructing their own versions of the story using their imaginations, spiritualities and experience. I have given an example of this in Chapter 2.[48]

An important question concerns the validity of both stories. Which version is superior? Is Group A's 'official' version superior? They, after all, had full information? But what about Group B? They had to use their own experience to construct their own story, using the fragments they had been given.

An important issue, arising from this exercise, is the question of legitimacy. It was once the case, in fact, it may still be the accepted belief, that the 'story' and the meaning of the faith and that of the church had one fixed meaning for all people. Individuals or particular groups who possess greater knowledge, education and learning, experience and training, are often deemed to be in fuller possession of the story, and are duly authorized to expound and interpret it. Others, not so well educated and trained, have to accept the version offered to them by their so-called 'betters'.

This point resonates with the work of a number of scholars who have looked at the whole question of epistemology (the philosophy of knowledge – how we know what we know). Our way of knowing and what we know, in addition to how seriously others view our knowledge, is often dependent upon who we are. The knowledge held by marginalized and oppressed peoples is often overlooked and disregarded.[49]

The important role undertaken by Group B lies in their attempt to tell their own story. The story has many meanings, and can be expressed in a variety of ways and in a variety of forms, depending upon experience and culture.

This liberating process begins with the most marginalized (Black children)[50] who, when encouraged to share their story, begin to redefine and liberate all people, especially those individuals in the centre, who represent the norm.

This exercise shows, also, the forms of legitimation that confer authority upon those in the first group, over and above those on the margins. In social scientific terms, researchers such as Altrichter et al. have commented upon a phenomenon which they have termed the 'hierarchy of credibility'.[51] In using the term 'hierarchy of credibility', the authors are speaking of a social ranking that confers a greater degree of credibility and reliability upon some people often at the expense of others. The latter are often perceived to have lesser status than the former. In the case of research within schools, the teacher is more 'reliable' than the pupil. The 'headteacher' is more reliable than the teacher.

A 'hierarchy of credibility' reinforces the truth-value of certain discourses and the legitimation of particular accounts. This hierarchy holds sway in the majority of churches, despite our gospel-based Kingdom theology which asserts the reversal of existing social norms and the need for leaders to be servants. Bishops or Chairs of Districts are often deemed more reliable or important than parish priests and circuit ministers. The latter, quite naturally, are more important than lay people. Qualified lay people have greater authority than those who have not been trained on pre-scribed or recognized courses. This implicit or explicit hierarchy simply reinforces the wider secular values of power, influence and importance. When the marginalized are given the power to challenge the norm the radicalism of the gospel is manifested in a manner that has greater authenticity for all.

Black youth (and older members of the community) need to be empowered to tell and share their own stories – in worship, in the teaching and learning life of the church, in the decision-making processes and in the celebratory life of the faith community. In all these areas, Black youth need to be involved, if they are truly to become a full part of the community.

'Redefining the norm' relates to a strategic method that allows churches to redefine the central norms that govern their life. This redefinition uses the most marginalized (Black youth) and the accompanying Christian education work that relates to these young members of the church as the catalyst in the liberating process. The teaching and learning materials, the work with Black youth in inner-city churches, became the primary means of liberating marginalized people in the church.

This process of 'redefining the norm', changing the existing ways in which the church defines itself, has been demonstrated to a varying degree within the churches that played a central role in this study. In these inner-city churches, the attempt to create a new model for a Black Christian education of liberation has given rise to innovative developments in worship and learning. Working initially with young people, these developments, if replicated across the whole of the church, can begin to liberate other marginalized people.

For example, older Black people, White working-class people, and women (especially Black women) may be affirmed and encouraged to use their talents and share their experiences in worship and in the life of the church. They will gain confidence when they see Black youth being given opportunity to express themselves.

In Fig. 4.2 the most powerful (the ones who define the 'norm') are located in the innermost ring. The least powerful are located outside the rings within the large octagon that surrounds all the other shapes. In figurative terms, 'redefining the norm' represents the movement of the powerless, the marginalized and the oppressed from the outer spaces of the octagon into the very centre of the inner ring. This movement, for many Black and liberation theologians, represents the authentic action (praxis) of the gospel of Christ, and the reordering of the usually exclusive rules that exist in a discriminatory world. In effect, this diagram represents the subversive work of the Kingdom of God.

The Pentecost service[52] at the Methodist church that played a central role in the study, and the harvest service at the same church, are important examples of how one might implement a new model for the Christian education of Black young people. The process of 'redefining the norm' was effected through the medium of these all-age acts of worship. These services, however, have also exerted a profound effect upon many adults. The inclusive and participative

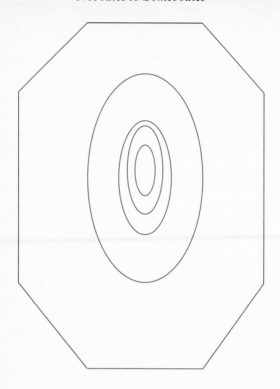

Fig. 4.2 'Redefining the norm'

nature of these African-centred acts of worship, which affirmed and
used Black cultures and experience, provided an opportunity for
many of the elders to express emotions and feelings that had been
internalized and suppressed for many years within the church.
'Redefining the norm' offers an important tool for the liberation of
all marginalized people in faith communities in Britain.

5

The Way it Should Be? Consolidating a Black Christian Education of Liberation

The final section, in the creative process that gave rise to *Growing into Hope*, was the four-week cycle of material for Lent and Easter. The writing of the material for Lent and Easter[1] owed much to the pioneering work of James Cone.

In adopting the theme of *Freedom*[2] I was concerned that the natural tendency to see the events of Easter Sunday in abstract spiritual terms should be dispelled. My aim was to create material that was both informed by and consistent with the central ideas and convictions of Black theology and transformative education.

When preparing the material for this four-week period, the recurrent themes of struggle, commitment and liberation were constantly to the fore. I am greatly indebted to James Cone, who enabled me to justify some of the more strident aspects of my theological reflection. Cone argues that God has sided with the oppressed peoples of the world through the particularity of Jesus Christ who came in a specific context as an oppressed Jew.[3] The implications for liberation are a corollary of this particular theological interpretation, and assume axiomatic qualities when applied to the life experiences of people of African descent. There is a need to fight the oppressive structures of White power and influence. This counter-struggle finds expression and legitimation in the theological understanding of God sending Jesus in order that oppressed and marginalized people might be free. Cone enlarges this point when he writes, 'Jesus is not a human being for all persons; he is a human being for oppressed persons, whose identity is made known in and through their liberation.'[4]

Cone continues by reminding us that the underlying philosophical principle governing human life is that of freedom. Human beings are created to be free, and that freedom is given theological substance in the Christian Gospels that detail the life, death and resurrection of Jesus.[5]

In a later work, Cone asserts that the person of Jesus Christ is inseparable from the quest for liberation and freedom.[6] Cone continues this point by stating:

> There is no liberation independent of Jesus' past, present, and future coming. He is the ground of our present freedom to struggle and the source of our hope that the vision disclosed in our historical fight against oppression will be fully realized in God's future. In this sense, liberation is not a human possession but a divine gift of freedom to those who struggle in faith against violence and oppression.[7]

The emphasis upon themes of freedom and liberation within Black theology encouraged me to construct teaching and learning materials that would assert the centrality of this concept within the whole educational strategy. More latterly, the work of Dwight Hopkins has been hugely influential, as he revisits Cone's work, putting the latter's thinking into a historical context. Hopkins' work confirmed in my own mind the efficacy of Black theology as basis for my theological reflection.[8]

Reflections on themes arising from the piloting of the *Lent* and *Easter* material: White normality and Black youth

An important theme that emerged from the latter section of the study was the reaction of Black youth to the Bible and their ideas of self and life. Black youth in this study seemed to require specific cultural frames of reference and African-centred indicators in order to perceive themselves and their identities positively (being legitimately represented). In a conversation with Malik, reflecting upon his exposure to the teaching and learning materials, I asked him about his perception of the people in the biblical narratives. I began by reminding Malik of the Pentecost session, which had been my first interaction with him. Using the material from Pentecost I showed Malik some of the pictures from this section of the material.[9]

ANTHONY (A):　I am going to show you some pictures now. These are a few things that were in the play as well. What do you think about them? So when like we did right, the play, one of the things we did, do you remember, was to show pictures of some of the people – people who were actually speaking in the actual play. So. [Shows Malik the picture, Appendix 12 in Volume 2] Do you remember that one?[10]

MALIK (M):　Yes.

A:　[Shows another picture, Appendix 13 in Volume 2] That picture?

M:　[Some hesitation] Yeah . . . That's a part of the play.

A:　So where do you think they come from?

M:　Africa?

A:　So when you, right, sort of read the Bible normally. If you close your eyes, right, and you actually imagine what the people look like, as well as reading it from a normal Bible, how would you imagine those people? [Pause while Malik thinks] OK. Let me test you here. Would you think that they look like you?

M:　No.

A:　What makes you say that?

M:　You can kinda tell what the person's like by the use of language. The way they speak. It kinda tells you. I mean, it doesn't ring a picture of someone like me when you read it straight out of the Bible.

A:　So, when you're reading about Pentecost, normally, alright? If I hadn't shown you the pictures and got you do the play from the book, how would you imagine the people?

M:　As White people. Yeah, I'd say that they were all White.

A:　And why would you say that?

M: 'Cos, if any of those people were Black yeah? We would know about it. Someone would have said.

One of the most important themes to emerge from this piloting process was the identification of self, with reference to biblical narratives and associated ideas of religious engagement. In my many encounters with Black youth, I was struck by their inability to construct positive, reflective images of self from what might be described as traditional, White-dominated Christian education material. In their own imaginings, without the added input of specific African-centred stimuli or cultural frames of reference, these individuals were unable to think of biblical characters in terms other than those associated with White Europeans. White Euro-centric constructs (or constructed ideas and understanding) are pervasive within historic-mainline churches. The power of such Eurocentric constructs prevented these Black youth from thinking in terms of sociocultural and family-based images that incorporated aspects of their own identity.

I had gained some awareness of this phenomenon from my previous interactions with the various groups. Despite my attempts to create material to address this issue,[11] I was still unaware of the depth and the complexity of this psychological malaise. My attempts at addressing this issue of psychological denial in the previous year had been based on an acknowledgement of the biased and self-serving nature of the pre- and post-colonial education of people of African descent.[12]

The literature pertaining to the education of peoples of African descent has many references to the negation of the Black psyche. The denial of the Black self emerged as a direct consequence of the self-serving educational processes that found expression in the epoch of slavery. This era in diasporan African history was followed, in turns, by extended periods of colonialization, which continue to this day in a variety of guises.

In addition to Woodson, writers such as Akbar, Coard, Kunjufu and Perkins[13] have all explored the area of Black miseducation. The works of these authors refer to the preponderance of negative imagery and the poor representation of African peoples in popular

and academic literature. Eze demonstrates that the negative representation of African peoples found full expression even in the
allegedly rational and objective world of the Enlightenment.[14]
These biased and self-serving philosophies became one of the primary means by which an all-embracing measure of psychological
control was exerted upon the African self.

The psychological repudiation of the Black self, implanted and
perpetuated by White power and authority, has led countless generations of Black people to see White as being superior to Black in
every sense. Working with these Black youth helped me to develop
a broader vision of the psychological battles that Black people need
to surmount if intellectual and emotional wholeness is to become a
reality. The children of the African diaspora have been exposed to
an ideological process of objectification,[15] in which they are represented in terms that are pejorative. Stuart Hall reminds us that there
is an inextricable link between representation and oppression.[16]

Dealing with White Eurocentric norms

The struggles of these Black youth, in this study, were not solely
confined to issues of Black negation and a negative representation.
In addition, there lay issues pertaining to the apparent normality of
White constructs. The concept of White has been established as
an all-pervasive norm. To counter this effect, these Black young
people required specific, intentional educational processes for their
emotional and psychological well being. In short, they needed additional educational and theological interventions that would assure
them that it was acceptable to be 'Black', or to be even more stark,
'non-White'. These new processes offer explicit permission for
such individuals to surmount the White Eurocentric ideas and
understanding that have exerted a measure of control over their
imagination.

Growing into Hope offered these young people an opportunity to
see aspects of their cultural and familial world reflected as the norm.
Engaging with them broadened my understanding. I witnessed the
need for Black youth to be exposed to African-centred material that

affirms the status of Black culture, existence and experience. The influence of White power and authority will lead Black children and young people to internalize their negative views of self. This is often placed alongside the perpetuation of White Eurocentric imagery that is constructed from material which, in theory, is described as being neutral or generic. Christian education material that is allegedly generic, neutral and universal, will almost always reinforce the status quo. Eurocentric ideas and understanding continue to dominate, and the images and visions that reflect African-centred experiences are perceived to lack validity.

A Black Christian education of liberation as a resource for self-esteem

The importance of Christian education, as a corrective to the ongoing psychological denial of the Black self, cannot be overstated. Christian education directed towards people of African descent must assert the importance of self-esteem. The teaching and learning process must be concerned with enabling Black people to have a profound appreciation and love of self. This self-love can be fostered by reminding Black youth that God, in whose image they are created, loves them and desires all that is good for their continued existence. Jawanza Kunjufu reminds us that:

> Self-esteem is enhanced by putting God first. 'If God be for us, who can be against us,' and 'greater is He in me than he who is in the world'. Placing God first in your life should provide greater strength for struggle against oppression. The problem with many religious people is reading only half the sentence, 'Love thy neighbour' – the remaining part is 'as thyself'. Many Black Christians love their neighbours better than they love themselves. [17]

Romney Moseley argues that by identifying and surrendering self to God, a person can begin to transcend the finite limitations of the self, in order to appreciate that God, through Jesus Christ, has transformed the world. [18] Ellison, like Moseley, seeks to fuse the discipline of developmental psychology with an interpretative approach (or hermeneutic) that is a common feature of theological inquiry. He argues that positive self-esteem does not come through self-denial. Rather, it is located in the recognition of God's unconditional love for us, and in the relationship that a person builds with God.[19]

In creating the material for Lent and Easter, I was anxious to develop themes, and an accompanying content, which would enable Black young people to identify with the incarnation of Jesus.[20] I wanted to develop a practical means of enabling Black youth to be affirmed in their cultural heritage. In short, I wanted to assist these individuals to embrace and celebrate those experiences that have been pivotal in shaping their identity. By enclosing a picture of a Black Jesus accompanied by the words, 'Jesus Loves Me – I am Free'[21] I wanted to assert, in inclusive terms, one of the basic convictions that underpins Black theology, namely, the concept of existential freedom! Understanding, accepting and embracing this prophetic statement is essential for the development of a positive sense of self.

The impact of the teaching and learning materials upon Black youth in the study: being and belonging in church

Through an ongoing series of observations I witnessed the influence of this educational process on Black young people. I was intrigued at how this teaching strategy had made a crucial impact on Black youth and their understanding of being in church.

In my conversation with Malik, I was fascinated by his reactions to the various sessions in which he had participated. I asked Malik about some of his perceptions from the different sessions.

ANTHONY (A):   So, when you were reading the play, that time at Pentecost. If I hadn't shown you the pictures, how would you imagine the people?

MALIK (M):   The same roughly.

A: Roughly the same?

M: Dressed in African clothing and stuff like that.

A: What made you think that?

M: Because of the way they were speaking to one another and stuff like that.

A: So, did that make the play more interesting?

M: Yes. 'Cos you wanted to hear what else was going to happen next. The people looked liked us, and they sounded like us, as well.

A: So, did you actually find that session, interesting?

M: Yeah, I liked it.

A: I mean, when like you were reading it out and it had lots of slang and modern language. Were you surprised when you started reading it?

M: Yeah! We've never done anything like that before.

Malik was excited about the various Sunday school/junior church sessions. These newly developed sessions were interactive and dialogical examples of the teaching and learning process. This methodology, coupled with an African-centred content, enlivened the usual process of Christian education in these churches. At a later point in our conversation I asked Malik about his interaction with the study.

A: So in terms of the activity [in the Palm Sunday material for the 'Middle' group],[22] in terms of, like, making decisions, how did you find that one?

M: Oh, yeah. Some of the questions were a bit difficult. 'Cos, like you had different parts saying yes and no. I like that.

A: What was good about it?

M: It's was like, errm, asking you what you would like to do and your thoughts. It left the choices and the decisions up to you. That was really hard, actually.

A: Looking back at Pentecost and something like the first activity you did last year with the play and then this stuff here, and the stuff you did last week. Overall, how would you say that was different from what you normally do?

M: Hmmnn. Because people want to do it. It's enjoyable, 'cos we can relate to it. And because we can relate to it, we remember it as well.

A: Over the past year or so. I know it's difficult to remember but, what would you say have been like the best moments in church, if any?

M: Yeah, when you've come. 'Cos, errmm like, we've wondered when you're coming. Like sometimes we ask when you're coming again. To do more plays and that. We enjoyed the Pentecost so much that we actually did that one again. Yeah, we did that one. In, errm, a Caribbean evening. We did that play.

A: Oh really? Right! How did it go down?

M: We enjoyed that. It was great.

In our conversations it was patently clear that Malik enjoyed interacting with the teaching and learning materials and the sessions. I was struck by Malik's sense of excitement at being involved in this process. The clarity of his recall when asked to reflect upon particular sessions was most impressive, given that a number of these events had taken place some twelve months previously. For Malik coming to church had become a more enjoyable and worthwhile exercise since he had become involved with the study.

One can point to examples of improved and changed practice in Christian education in this Methodist church, situated towards the western end of the city. This is evidenced in the ability of this faith community to integrate elements of the culture and experience of Black people within the wider corporate life of the church. This is manifested, for example, in the existence of Caribbean evenings. Black youth are beginning to be incorporated at the very heart of this intergenerational community of faith.

This church is beginning to make the transition from a body that is governed solely by overarching Eurocentric norms to a community that appreciates the importance of Black cultural experiences and expressions of faith.

One needs to put these developments into some perspective, however, by acknowledging the continued presence of White,

Eurocentric values and aesthetics, which continue to dominate this and the majority of historic-mainline churches in Britain. *Growing into Hope* has made a difference. It remains the case, however, that these interventions along with such initiatives as Caribbean evenings remain nothing more than small additions in the ongoing life of this church. The traditional centre of operations that govern this faith community remained largely unchanged. If one wished to be overly critical, it could be argued that in the intervening time since this research was first conducted, a number of the churches have not improved their practice. On the contrary, they have regressed, back into their old stupefying and restrictive Eurocentric practices that fail to reflect their historical and contemporary experiences as people of African descent.

Despite the piecemeal efforts of many of the churches to create inclusive, African-centred acts of worship and learning, one can report a positive reaction from Black youth to the relatively few examples that have emerged. The affirmation, self-esteem and sense of belonging conferred upon Black youth when they are given opportunities to play significant parts within the whole worshipping life of the church cannot be overstated. This has been a recurrent theme within the study.

The necessity to surmount the dichotomy between worship[23] and learning[24] has important generic considerations for all churches. Historic-mainline churches in Britain have exuded the seemingly blithe belief that children are too young to worship, while adults are too old to learn.[25] This belief has become almost enshrined, in seemingly axiomatic terms, within many of these faith communities.

This apparent belief is manifested in the practice of many churches, and has led to the continuing marginalization of children and to a lesser extent, young people, from the powerful reality of worship within the central life of the faith community.[26]

If this misconception is permitted to continue, there remains the danger that these faith communities will be presiding over a potentially ruinous situation. The alienation and disaffection of young people will remain a self-perpetuating weakness within historic-mainline churches.

Jeff Astley argues that Christian maturity is found through the psychological reality of growing into Christ, whose person we are asked to imitate. The most effective setting in which these attitudinal changes may occur is the worshipping community.[27]

Developing Black leadership through intergenerational worship and learning

With specific reference to children of African descent, I would assert that there are additional, compelling reasons for Black youth to be nurtured (and inculturated) within the whole worshipping life of the church. It is my belief that a sense of affirmation and self-esteem can be instilled in Black youth by providing them with early opportunities for leadership. This process can be facilitated by exposing such individuals to the transcendent elements of worship, and mutuality with peers and elders. As Avery Dulles argues, participation within the whole life of the church and the wider community for people of all ages is of crucial importance.[28] The importance of exposing children to the transcendent elements of worship has been a concern for those who exercise national responsibility for children's work in British churches.[29]

Michael Clarke, in his research amongst Black youth in Barbados, ascribes his own success in academic terms to the acute sense of belonging he derived from being within the Anglican Church of Barbados. Clarke never had cause to doubt the psychological reality of God's love for him.[30] Romney Moseley argues that the next generation of Black leadership in the United States must emerge from Black youth, who are nurtured and taught within an intergenerational framework, cocooned in the affirming and dynamic auspices of the Black church.[31]

Historic-mainline churches need to affirm and empower Black youth. These young people will become Black leaders of the future. These energized, empowered young people are needed to sustain Black-majority, inner-city faith communities. Their empowerment has to be achieved through concerted efforts to incorporate and affirm the worshipping presence of Black youth within the church. Black youth must be empowered, if they are to move from the often marginalized areas of Sunday school/junior church into the very heart of the worshipping community. Through their increased participation, these young people may begin to develop the necessary confidence and skill to confront the barriers of racism that lie ahead of them, within the church and the wider society. Moreover, their very presence will liberate the whole community of faith.

Consultations with Black youth

In order to gain further information on the experiences and thoughts of Black youth I organised a small informal conference, in which pertinent issues concerning the presence of Black youth in historic-mainline churches could be discussed. This conference was a collaborative piece of work, with the organization of the event being shared between two Black Christian youth workers and myself. It was agreed that the conference would take place at the Methodist church that had become a central player in the study. The conference was initially aimed at young Black Methodists, but was later widened to incorporate Black young people from neighbouring inner-city churches across the city of Birmingham.

The creation of this conference arose from the entreaties of several African-Caribbean young people, with whom I had worked closely throughout the study. Many of these young people felt isolated from the churches with which they were identified.

The conference was an opportunity for the young people to participate and share in an affirming environment. It was the hope of the adult facilitators that this conference might be free from the limitations of mimicked Christian behaviour and self-conscious religiosity, characteristics that tend to predominate when people attend church on a Sunday. In order to discourage these tendencies the conference was scheduled to take place on a Saturday. By changing the day, it was hoped that a more critically reflective conversation relating to the experiences of being a young Black person in church might emerge. Concurrent with the desire for a critically reflective discussion was my hope to gain further insights into the impact of *Growing into Hope* on these young people.

The resulting discussion provided me with an important theme that was to shape the final phase of the study. A number of the young people spoke about the seeming inability of the church and the wider society to change. They reiterated their belief that the church was unwilling to change. It was felt that the church and wider British society was irredeemably racist. Not only could the church not change, but its response, and that of the nation as a whole, was one of patronizing and controlling the actions of Black people, and then making them the scapegoats for their struggles and hardships.

This sense of resignation, in response to the seeming immutability of the church, and the nation as a whole, gave rise to a great deal of further reflection and analysis on my part. I developed a theory and an accompanying training exercise in order that this issue might be described clearly, for the benefit of Black youth and the many individuals who assisted them in their Christian education and nurture. What resulted from these initial reflections is a potentially important theory, which has consequences for historic-mainline churches and wider British society.

The development of what I have termed a 'theology of good intentions' has its origins in my doctoral research, which constitutes the greater part of this book. Much of the thinking that follows, however, was undertaken after the initial research. I am indebted to a number of colleagues and many Black young people, whose thoughts and comments have enabled me to develop this work further.

So what is a 'theology of good intentions'?

A 'theology of good intentions' is a phenomenon that I (along with many other Black people) have lived with for many years. I have coined the term 'good intentions' as a way of reflecting the dynamics of this phenomenon. In the first instance, a 'theology of good intentions' has emerged from the countless occasions when, as a Black person, I have been on the end of some thoughtless and insulting words, expressions, actions or behaviour. I have witnessed these examples or incidents all my life, but the catalyst for this line of thought arose from an unfortunate incident at the Methodist Conference a number of years ago.[32] What I remember most clearly about that incident is the number of people who, following the incident and the resulting apology, demanded that I 'rise above' the whole thing and empathize with the other person. While I was being advised to be a good forgiving Christian, I wondered what injunctions were being placed upon the other person?

The term a 'theology of good intentions' was first coined following my reflections upon that initial incident. As I reflected upon similar incidents of the present and the past, the term became increasingly real. I thought about every occasion, when despite repeated pleas and assurances, the same offences, oversights and injustices were perpetrated against Black and minority ethnic people. I thought about the many occasions when complaints were made by Black people in response to these constant *mistakes* or *unfortunate* incidents. In response to our pleas, the inevitable reply was always a simple apology. The comments or incidents were never intended. It was always a mistake, and 'sorry' was the appropriate, indeed the only response to yet another unfortunate event. A 'theology of good intentions' is a way of responding to situations of injustice, in which the perpetrator fails to take full responsibility for their actions. It is a way of responding to the oppressed and powerless, by refusing to take the experiences or perspectives of these people seriously. Rather than deal with the reasons for their actions, they are content to settle for the type of rhetoric that claims 'I didn't mean it, I am sorry'. The last phrase (a mantra for those who constantly issue it) has been used so often, I began to think that it might be infused with magic properties. No one has ever meant to cause offence. It is always an accident. The intentions of the people who issue the apology cannot be challenged. In fact, their intentions are *always* good. The accidental nature of these events would be less offensive, however, if they were not repeated on a regular basis.

A 'theology of good intentions' – a way of reading the Bible

The source for a 'theology of good intentions' is found in the paternalistic and patrician attitude that is often manifested in the life of historic-mainline churches and in wider British society. This attitude flows from a particular narrow reading of the Bible, coupled with a limited understanding of God. A 'theology of good intentions' is an attempt to separate a vengeful and angry God of the Old Testament from the more pietistic and emollient view of the divine that is reflected in the life, death and resurrection of Jesus, in the New Testament. It is a way of identifying with God only in terms of the latter. Of equal importance, it is a particularly narrow view of Jesus.

A 'theology of good intentions' cannot come to terms with a God who will chastise, punish and rebuke. This God is neutral. A God that is transcendent, beyond the sufferings and injustices of creation. Certainly, this God cannot be understood in a liberationist sense, where the Creator actively intervenes on the side of the oppressed and marginalized.

A 'theology of good intentions' stands in marked contrast to the existence and experiences of African people, particularly, in the way we pray, which incorporates an understanding that God can answer prayer in a literal, interventionist fashion.[33]

A 'theology of good intentions' attempts to create a convenient dichotomy between the God of the Old Testament and the God of the New. This dichotomy is extended by encouraging Christian discipleship to identify with a privatized, spiritualized notion of the New Testament God, at the expense of a corporate, decisive God of the Old. A cursory look at the passages within most lectionaries and schemes for Christian education reveals an apparent imbalance between the mythical narratives[34] of the Hebrew Bible, and the stories of Jesus, as presented in the Gospels.

Even when New Testament stories are invoked, the liberating, challenging polemic of the narrative is de-emphasized, in order that the prophetic and challenging and judging nature of Scripture might be overlooked. In effect, a moderate, status quo laden form of approach (hermeneutic) is used. One that fossilizes biblical narrative in a particular time and space removed from our own, where the truths to be discerned are essentially spiritual, not political or ideological. Hence, the deliverance of the Israelites from Egypt (Ex. 6–13) is the story of God's faithfulness and is not to be understood either as a narrative of liberation, or as a denunciation of oppressive Egyptian rule. To understand it as either liberationist or denunciation is not in keeping with a 'theology of good intentions'.

A 'theology of good intentions': identifying with Jesus

This theology owes much to our perception of Jesus as depicted in the Gospels. The Jesus with whom we identify is often the 'gentle Jesus, meek and mild' of our childhood prayers and Christian education and nurture in Sunday school. It is a Jesus 'Who never said a mumbling word' in the face of his detractors. It is a view of Jesus where the overturning of the tables in the temple is either a temporary aberration, or can be explained away in pious terms with the well-worn phrase, 'righteous anger', i.e., this is not the normal behaviour of Jesus (that is reserved for the 'meek and mild' version), but is one exception that would seem to link Jesus with a not so pleasant Old Testament God. It is a Jesus who has been held captive and colonized in the service of White, Eurocentric ideology and power. This version of Jesus is a construction of the Victorian age and the syrupy image portrayed in numerous Christian education curricula of that era, and the early part of the twentieth century.

Reversing the natural relationship between the offender and the offended

Central to the workings of a 'theology of good intentions' is the subversion and reversal of the normal modes of responsibility. By steadfastly refusing to acknowledge the relationship between power, injustice and oppression, those who constantly invoke a 'theology of good intentions' are able to use the rhetoric of apology as the dominant motif in this form of discourse.

By issuing repeated apologies, the locus of responsibility is shifted from the oppressor to the oppressed. The responsibility for healing any resulting breaches or discord rests with the recipient of the injustice, not with the perpetrator. Continual complaint by the recipient of such abuses is to earn the sobriquet of 'troublemaker'. In effect, Black people become the problem, not issues of injustice or systemic and systematic abuses of power. I have lost count of the number of occasions that, resulting from a dispute between a White person with power and a Black person in a subordinate position, the final recourse has been to simply move the Black person. In such situations no resulting or further action was taken against the person with or in power. In effect the Black person *was the problem*. Jacquelyn Grant, writing with reference to this situation comments thus,

> Part of the tendency to negate the humanity of some peoples may be seen in the corresponding tendency to locate the blame for their situation on those who have been dehumanized. Hence, we hear the familiar question: What is wrong with blacks, or women or youth? What is their problem? Although these questions often have been asked, they are inappropriate questions. The victims are blamed for situations and conditions over which they have no control.[35]

The truth of Grant's words can be seen in the tired, racialized debates which surround the whole area of immigration and so-called 'race relations' in Britain. The justification for punitive immigration laws is based upon the seemingly commonsense notion of limiting the numbers of non-White people in Britain. By limiting the numbers, so it is argued, we limit the potential for 'race' conflict, and thereby create a conducive environment for good 'race rela-tions'. This logic, such as it exists, is based on the notion that Black people per se are the problem, not the existing racist and xeno-phobic attitudes that have been endemic in Britain for over a thousand years. This is classic 'theology of good intentions'. Black

people may be the recipients of racial attacks and abuse but, funda-
mentally, it is their fault – first, for being Black and second, for
having the temerity to be in this country.

The notion of sorrow rather than repentance

A 'theology of good intentions' is predicated upon the notion that
'sorry' is the right and only response to issues of injustice and
marginalization. It matters less that the conditions that give rise to
such oppression and marginalization are often untouched or remain
unchallenged. Systemic abuses and institutionalized racism are
often disguised within the all-embracing veneer of the rhetoric of
the apology.

The individuals who refuse to accept the continuing apologies of
the ones who committed the initial offence, are deemed to be people
who have 'chips on their shoulders', or possess 'attitude problems'.
On occasions, the words of a passive and supine Jesus are liberally
invoked, reminding such malcontents that they are to 'turn the
other cheek' (Luke 6.29). Forgiveness in response to the ubiquitous
'sorry' is the order of the day, but little, if anything, is said concerning justice and repentance.

Once the word 'sorry' is invoked, it is expected to suffice, with no
accompanying recognition of the incident or situation until the next
apology is issued. Often, a further apology is made for the same
oversight that was committed previously. Failure to forgive, or to
collude in this unhealthy and unhelpful scenario, is to earn the
disapproval of those who committed the offence in the first instance.
The recipient is often condemned for being 'unchristian'. The
words, 'Now would Jesus have done that?' are used to validate the
actions of the ones who committed the offence in the first instance.

The sentiment of sorrow is surgically removed from the injustice
and systemic inequalities that rendered the apology necessary. A
'theology of good intentions' is predicated on a passive, forgiving
notion of God – a God who will not condemn or call to account. As
James Cone informs us, a supine God who is without wrath is not a
God one would naturally associate with liberation. This God is one

who will legitimize the status quo.[36] Clearly, Cone, as a Black liberation theologian, opposes this particular understanding of God. Cone argues that Black and oppressed peoples have no use for a God that does not condemn or stand alongside the marginalized in solidarity.[37] Using a 'theology of good intentions' one is able to read the narrative of Luke 19.1–10, without ever recognizing that Zacchaeus, as part of his repentance (not just sorrow), makes recompense for his former actions. He repays those he has treated unfairly (*reparations* might be an appropriate term to use) and establishes a new relationship between the wronged and the wrongdoer.

A 'theology of good intentions' is manifested in a myriad different environments and contexts. It is exhibited in a number of inner-city churches in which I have worked in a variety of ways. Chief amongst them is the exercising of power and authority within the church.

Within a number of the historic-mainline, inner-city churches, I have been aware of the existence of a small group of influential, White middle-class professionals. These individuals, courtesy of their education and standing in the wider society (through professions such as teaching, social work, the law, local government, etc.), exert a disproportionate amount of influence upon the church. Their influence upon the church is often at the expense of Black members.

Moving beyond a 'theology of good intentions': the challenge for a Black Christian education of liberation

Initial reflections on two human encounters

In order to illustrate the realities of a 'theology of good intentions', first let me offer you two stories. Two human encounters which I hope will put this phenomenon, and the theory that accompanies it, into some kind of context. These stories have emerged from the life experiences of Black young people in Britain. In light of the death of Stephen Lawrence and the Macpherson report, they are, I believe, a timely reminder of the pernicious nature of racism in Britain. A 'theology of good intentions' should be seen in the context of Stephen Lawrence's death, and the actions and attitudes of the machinery of the British police and the criminal and judicial systems.

The first of the two events occurred a number of years ago, back in the summer of 1993. I was employed at that time as a church-related youth and community worker for two inner-city Methodist churches in the north-west area of Birmingham. My work was primarily with African-Caribbean young people between the ages of seven and eighteen. One morning I received a phone call from a distraught mother. Her sixteen-year-old son had been arrested on his way to school where he was to take a GCSE exam.

Arriving at the local police station in the area, I was informed by the arresting officer that this young man had been detained, as he matched the description of a Black youth that had allegedly carried out a mugging on an elderly man, out walking his dog. In addition to pleading his innocence (he had irrefutable evidence to verify his whereabouts at the time the incident took place), the young man informed the officer that he was on his way to school to take an exam. The police officer remained unmoved at the youth's entreaties. The young man was arrested and consequently missed his exam. After a delay of a few hours, when the necessary phone calls had been made to verify the young man's story, he was released. By this time, of course, he had missed his exam. No charges were ever brought against this Black youth. No action was ever taken against the officer. No apology was ever made. The examination board refused to take his exceptional circumstances into account and he was not given any award. It was to be a number of months before he could finally take the exam.

The belated apologies that were subsequently made by the police force and the examination board were somewhat hollow. It was, of course, not their fault. As the Black youth was not at fault either, save for the obvious crime of being Black, it would appear that no one was at fault. White authority apologized, but no inquiry was made, and no one was called to account. No judgement was made on the officer. The incident was forgotten by the institutional powers that be – until the next such event. That Black youth has not forgotten that incident.

The second event concerns another Black youth from the same church. This event occurred some two years after the one described in the previous story. This Black young man, aged sixteen, was accompanying a group of friends from his church youth club to a prestigious national Christian youth event. There he became separated from the rest of the group. His ticket, for entry into the venue they had arranged to attend, was held by one of the youth leaders. The young man approached one of the many door stewards and asked that they make an announcement in order to alert the youth leader of his presence outside the venue. The steward refused. The Black young man remonstrated, arguing that he was part of a bone fide youth group, and that his youth leader was inside the venue. One message and a subsequent announcement could have resolved the situation. The White door steward flatly refused. The Black youth was an undesirable interloper who must be repelled. Not only did the steward not carry out request of the Black youth, he instead instructed a colleague to call for the police. The police arrived and removed the Black youth.

Once again, after a delay of a few hours, the matter was cleared up. The youth leader arrived and confirmed the young man's story. This was not before the Black youth had spent over two hours in a police station having missed the event in question. As in the previous story, apologies were issued and promises made. Questions were asked, but no satisfactory answers were given. In a sense of anger, outrage and bitterness, the Black youth left the Christian youth club, vowing never to return. Two brief vignettes; two real life events; two disillusioned and disaffected young men; two individuals who have experienced the full brunt of a 'theology of good intentions'.

Educational strategies for responding to a 'theology of good intentions'

The problems posed by a 'theology of good intentions' are real. How can Black people, particularly Black youth, be enabled to challenge the constant struggles of finding the appropriate responses to issues of injustice, unfairness and oppression? Responding to and overcoming a 'theology of good intentions' demands a number of creative strategies.

The following exercise is an attempt, on my part, to put some flesh onto the bones of this theory. 'Who is Invited to the Party?' was created as a means of enabling Black young people to engage in a creative process which helps them deal effectively with the problems of being excluded and pathologized. This exercise has been developed to enable Black youth and the many practitioners who support them in their development to understand the workings of a 'theology of good intentions'.

The exercise: 'Who is Invited to the Party?'

- Divide the group into two halves. Ask one half of the group to walk to the right-hand side of the room and the other group to walk to the left-hand side.

- Inform both groups that you will be holding a party on the first Friday of each month. As the one who has ultimate power and authority, you are in a position to decide who will be coming to your party.

- You inform the group on the right that they will be invited to the party. Every Friday they will be asked to attend your party.

- You inform the group on the left that they will also be invited to your party. Every Friday they will be asked to attend your party.

- Inform both groups that a week has gone by. You had the party on the Friday, but you forgot to invite the group on the right to your party on the Friday as you had promised. You fully intended to, but you simply forgot. How do they feel hearing this news? The group on the left were invited and many of them attended the party.

- Having apologized to the group on the right and promised them that they will be invited to the next party, you remind the group on the left that they are also invited to the party.

- You inform both groups that another week has passed and that you forgot to invite the group on the right once again. You fully intended to, but once again, you forgot. The group on the left attended the party once again. How does the group on the right feel, having been promised, but then overlooked when the party took place? How does the group on the left feel, having attended the party in the knowledge that others were excluded?

- Repeat the above operation on another five or six occasions. How does the group on the right feel? What about the group on the left? Does the group on the left feel at an advantage, having been able to actually attend the party? Do they feel guilty at all? Should they have stayed away from the party in solidarity? Make a note of the reactions of both groups. At what point does the group on the right become totally disaffected by this inequitable process?

Reflections on the exercise

The exercise has been linked to Luke's account of the wedding feast (Luke 14.7–14) and the issue concerning who sits in the prominent seats at the 'party'. Jesus proceeds to ask even more telling questions concerning who should be invited to the party in the first instance. The relevance of this passage to the exercise and the resulting reflections should be self-evident.

The above exercise is intended to represent the church and British society, and their attempts to accommodate and include Black and minority ethnic people within the faith community and nation at large. In a great number of respects, Black people are denied full access to the whole life of the church and society. This sense of denial is manifested in the inability of Black people to bring their innate gifts and their authentic selves into church and society. The two groups in the exercise represent Black and White people, particularly White people who hold office and exercise power and authority.

The group on the left represents the many White middle-class people. These people are promised a place at the party and the invitation duly arrives and they are able to attend the party. The person issuing the invitation ensures that these people are represented at the party. This is undoubtedly the case for White middle-class people in both church and society. It would be inconceivable that this group should be excluded from either setting.

The group on the right is somewhat more complex. In some respects, the fact that these people (who are representative of Black people and their experiences in this country) have actually been issued with an invitation to the party represents a marked sense of progress in itself. For many Black people, who were part of the first generation of mass migrants to Britain from the Caribbean, post-1945, were not offered overwhelming welcomes, and not invited unequivocally to be a part of the church and the wider society. Not only were they not welcomed, on many occasions they were told explicitly to leave the church. Far Right organizations, such as the National Front, made the case for them to leave the country as a whole. The actions of the host of the party towards the group on the right represent the more contemporary attitude – the attitude that prevails today. This is the attitude of good intentions. It is one that always attempts to do the right thing. It is the attitude that has its heart in the right place. Yet, as we saw from the exercise, it does not progress much further than rhetoric. The people, to whom the promises are made, never find themselves at the party on the Friday. Whether the host accidentally forgot, or whether it was a conscious decision, is largely irrelevant, because, either way, these people still find themselves outside of the party.

Eventually, over a period of time, the group on the right will become tired of hearing the seemingly hollow promises of the host. They will most likely refuse to listen to the empty entreaties and will decide for themselves that they do not want to attend the party at all, even if a later invitation is a genuine one. It is the case that Black people have grown tired of the many promises made by the church and by society, and subsequently decided that they are no longer interested in being included in the heart of either body or corporate entity. These Black people feel they have been let down too often, and do not wish any longer to listen to continued promises of change in practice.

The church and the wider society, in all its decision-making processes and ways of operating, must attempt to move away from a culture and a 'theology of good intentions'. They must find ways of delivering on the rhetoric of the immediate and distant past. They must have strategies and policies that can be implemented. Monitoring should be in order, to ensure that those promises are being put into effect, and are seen to be working. If not, then the fine words and promises will remain just that, and Black people will continue to find themselves elsewhere when the party is taking place, despite the warm platitudes.

The realities I have outlined, in this section, offer a clear rationale and a justification for Black support and empowerment groups, within Methodism and in other historically White-dominated churches. These movements are not reverse forms of racism. Alternatively, they should be seen as much needed strategies to enable Black people to remain within larger institutions, which are often racially oppressive. In answer to those who want to put forward the charge of 'reverse discrimination', my usual response is, 'What would you prefer? That the church although uncomfortable with such support systems and initiatives continues to support their existence, or Black and minority ethnic people leave? You can't have it both ways?' It seems to me that some White Christians cannot make up their minds about what they want. They are more concerned with how things appear and the niceties of procedure (Black people meeting separately is seen as an 'unhelpful' development) rather than displaying any interest in exploring the reasons why Black people feel the need to create these support networks in order to remain a part of the church. In effect, our efforts to deal with a 'theology of good intentions' are more offensive than the very existence of racism itself.

This 'theology of good intentions' becomes all the more pernicious for the effects it has upon the recipient. On a number of occasions when this exercise has been enacted, there has been a common response from one particular group of participants. Those playing the host (especially if they are White Europeans) have become indignant at the refusal of the invitees who have been continually shunned to acknowledge the good faith of those who are issuing the invite, namely themselves.

'Who Is Invited to the Party?' and the reflections that accompany it are my attempt to construct a teaching strategy that will enable Black youth to gain an understanding of the importance of such resources as critical thinking, recollection and repetition. The exercise challenges Black youth to construct strategies by which they effectively challenge the half-truths and doubtful motives of the host.

When the exercise has been enacted, a variety of strategies have been employed by Black young people to challenge the 'good intentions' of the host. Amongst the most creative of these has been to organize one's own party, a party that is so vibrant and attractive that the existing, exclusive party will feel threatened and even lose popularity with its existing client group. One could argue that this process has been exemplified in western societies by the ongoing popularity of hip-hop music in general and Black expressive cultures, particularly popular culture in general.[38] When we are excluded and marginalized, we often do our thing and soon that 'thing' becomes the standard barometer for all that is vibrant and authentic.

Using theological and educational resources for overcoming a 'theology of good intentions'

As a Black Christian educator and practical theologian, I am primarily concerned with developing teaching and learning strategies by which Black people, particularly Black youth, can recognize themselves to be created, spiritual beings, in the image of God. As such, I am concerned that we develop strategies and approaches that enhance our capacity to be all that we can and should be. In this respect, I will attempt to map out the basic tenets and strategies of a new approach to Christian education that will enable Black young people in Britain to respond creatively to a 'theology of good intentions'.

In the first instance, a strategy that attempts to empower Black people to move beyond a 'theology of good intentions' is one that asserts the importance of affirming one's basic identity and self-image.[39]

The first step towards surmounting the negative effects of a 'theology of good intentions' is the constant reminder that *all people* are created in God's image and are, in effect, the summit of God's creative powers for the world God brought into being. Craig Ellison argues that self-esteem and a sense of affirmation are to be found in the realization of God's unconditional love for humankind.[40]

Having attempted to describe the central importance of affirmation and self-esteem, it is essential for the well-being of Black people that we begin to construct theoretical and practical strategies for challenging and subverting this 'theology of good intentions'. I would like to posit an alternative perspective for enabling Black people, particularly young people, to overcome the pressures that are associated with a 'theology of good intentions'.

The importance of dialogue

In this respect the theory and practice of transformative education has much to teach us, particularly when applied to the realms of theological reflection. In Chapter 3, I outlined the importance of dialogue in Black theological reflection. This approach is one that incorporates critical reflection upon experience, linked to a Black interpretative approach to reading the Bible (a Black hermeneutic). Through this process, I believe that Black young people can be encouraged to engage in a process of situational analysis[41] (analysing their lives and the context in which they live), in order to interrogate their present experience for its truthfulness.[42]

This form of critical reflection upon events can assist Black young people to negotiate the divide between stoical inaction and often naïve and simplistic recourses to violence. The aim is not to encourage Black youth to be passive, stoical or conformist. Yet, this strategy of rereading and reflecting remains crucial, if Black young people are to negotiate the hazards of being Black in a racist society. In short, how could the Black youths in the two stories we read previously have negotiated their way through the perilous waters in which they both found themselves?

The importance of critical thinking and reflection is not a new phenomenon. It can be argued that African people have engaged in individual and collective reflection from our earliest times. During the immediate post Second World War struggles of New Commonwealth migrants in Britain, the basis for survival was often through a plethora of communal and interpersonal support networks.[43] One of my earliest memories of growing up in an African-Caribbean home in Bradford was of my parents' home being invaded by many people, who came by the house to 'drop their pardner' on a Sunday afternoon.[44] An important feature of these visits were the habitual conversations about events that had taken place within the Black community of Bradford at that time.

Within Rastafari, the term 'reasoning' has been used to evoke the notion of collective contemplation and reflection upon present and historic experiences.[45] Joseph Crockett identifies Psalm 137 in the Hebrew scriptures, and the notion of 'exile', as being fundamental to the analytical and reflective processes of African Americans, when meditating upon their past and present struggles.[46]

Given the importance of reflection and critical thinking, it is imperative that Black young people are afforded 'safe spaces' in which these processes can be learnt, rehearsed and practised, in order that they can be deployed when the next crisis situation should arise. In this context 'Black-majority' churches, of whatever guise, assume great importance. The practicalities of Black-majority churches providing a safe space for Black youth to rehearse and critically reflect upon issues pertaining to identity, selfhood, actualized faith and belonging, can be seen in a number of examples on both sides of the Atlantic. In the American context, there are the respective approaches of Michael Ross in South Carolina[47] and Jeremiah Wright[48] in Chicago.

Within the British context, there are the differing approaches of

Mike Vance,[49] Corrine Julius[50] and George Richards.[51] The latter have identified 'supplementary schools'[52] as important vehicles through which Black young people can gain positive measures of self-esteem and confidence, so vital if one is to overcome the worst excesses of a 'theology of good intentions'. These varying approaches to supplementary education are supported, to greater and lesser degrees, by Black-majority churches.

Recollection and repetition

Arising from the process of critical reflection is the notion of 'repetition'. Romney Moseley argues that reflection, in the first instance, is an integral aspect of being human. He writes,

> Authentic selfhood requires critical reflection. There is a shift from being acted on by the world and acting on the world. The question arises whether the self is constituted autonomously or by another.[53]

Moseley stresses that subsequent to critical reflection is the important task of recollection and repetition. These twin modes of critical thinking are framed in a unitary struggle, in order that the self can both remember that which has been, and to constantly replay that moment with a view to remaking it and refashioning it in the here and now.[54] Moseley, with reference to repetition, writes,

> As a metaphor from the theater, repetition is a 'retaking' or repeating what was previously enacted as if it were for the first time . . . But repetition is not merely the recovery of lost love. It is the recovery of lost selfhood, and selfhood is *essentially* a dialectical relationship between the finite and infinite.[55]

Within the literature of Black Christian education, a number of writers have worked with the notion of recollection and repetition. While the majority of these scholars have not brought the analytical insights of moral philosophy and psychology to the proceedings, in a manner that characterizes Moseley's work, they have, nonetheless, posited notions of repeated and re-enacted narrative within their work. Anne Wimberly stresses the importance of people of African descent revisiting corporate and familial narratives, and fusing these with Scripture in order to understand the past, affirm their selfhood in the present and, ultimately, to remake the future.[56]

Similarly, in her work with African-American adolescents, Evelyn Parker utilizes personal and archetypal narratives as a means of enabling the Black youth in her study to discern the liberative impulse that has remained the heartbeat of Black diasporan experience.[57]

The work of Wimberly and Parker dovetails with my own approaches to the task of recollection and repetition within the British context. I have sought, through the medium of familial narratives, to create a systematic approach to Christian education and nurture whereby Black youth can gain access to the historic developments of their experience and existence.[58] Exposure to this process can enable them to use these stories, as a means of distilling elements of the survival ethic, in order to remake and refashion their own futures.[59]

Returning for a moment to the front room of my parents' home in Bradford and the scene of numerous adults arguing over the events of the long distant and more immediate past, while they threw[60] their 'pardner', I am reminded of the importance of recollection and repetition. As I stood, watching these grown adults recount the same story countless times, my adolescent thinking constructed this scene as the repetitious ramblings of Black people who were simply old and stupid. They could not remember if they had shared this story before. Maybe they had spent too long in Britain, experiencing the fiery furnace of racism and disaffection?

In retrospect, perhaps, there was a deliberate, albeit unconscious, ploy to their discursive ramblings? Perhaps, they were engaging, in a process of recollection and repetition? The very stuff which I am advocating now? Perhaps they were sitting at the riverside, reflecting upon how they could sing the Lord's song in a strange land?[61] Thomas, Wimberly and Wimberly have commented on the importance of honouring and sharing the wisdom and fortitude of our elders.[62]

Dash, Jackson and Rasor assert that the sense of being for people of African descent (our ontological source of self) lies in the interconnectedness of our existence. In this particular idea, the finite and infinite, the self and the wider community, the global and the local, are linked by a vibrant African spirituality, which unites the disparate parts with the whole. That 'whole' is the heart of God.[63] The authors stress the importance of community, and intercommunal relationships, as being at the very heart of the African notion of existence – a resource that has empowered the African self in the diaspora.[64] The authors assert that at the heart of our corporate and individual notions of existence lies God, in whose image we are created and in whom and through whom we achieve our ultimate sense of belonging, affirmation and selfhood.[65]

Concluding thoughts on this matter – for now!

In responding to the phenomenon of a 'theology of good intentions', I have tried to utilize those resources and experiences that have accompanied Black people on their diasporan journeys, coupled with the notion of critical reflection. I hope that these developing approaches are ones that enable Black young people to challenge and ultimately overcome the 'theology of good intentions'.

Additional concerns and reflections from Black youth: the need for Black popular forms of music in inner-city historic-mainline churches

One of the primary complaints of the young people regarding the church was the issue of music. Of the young people's various concerns,[66] chief amongst them was the issue of music in the church. In my previous interaction with Black youth, the importance of Black expressive cultures and aesthetics was noted, as an important facet in the Christian education of these individuals. Writers such as Nelson Copeland have argued that any form of intervention directed at Black youth must recognize and offer constructive engagement with elements of Black culture.[67] William

Myers offers a contextual model for Black Christian urban youth work that acknowledges and affirms the importance of Black expressive cultures within worship.[68] The importance of Black expressive cultures, with particular reference to music, is a central feature of James Cone's seminal work that dates from the early 1970s.[69]

Black styles of music have an important role in implying identity, and providing an essential resource for engagement and belonging, within a faith community. This was amply demonstrated by my many conversations with these young people. One can gain a sense of the frustration at the lack of Black expressive music, in the church, from the following brief extract. Marlon is a young African-Caribbean male, fourteen years of age. I asked Marlon about the type of music he would like to hear in the church.

ANTHONY (A): What things would you want in your church?
MARLON (M): Better music.
A: What sort of music do you want?
M: More modern music.
A: Such as?
M: Modern music. Like you can put the type of church music that you wanna get, or put across to different generations with different bits, like putting traditional religious tunes to something like reggae.
A: Why would you like that kind of music in church?
M: Because it gets a point across in the same way but using a more modern approach. Because we're the next generation, so they're gonna have to look towards developing us into liking the church and seeing why the church is good for us. In order to do that they got to make us see; they got to show us why the church is good.

Robert Beckford reminds us that Black popular culture, in the form of music, has a long tradition within predominantly Black-led/Black-majority churches for denoting subversive forms of resistance to White authority.[70]

These young people were frustrated by the church's lack of engagement with Black popular forms of music. This failure, to my mind, is of crucial importance. There exists a discontinuity between

the wider world in which these young people exist and the seemingly enclosed and anachronistic world of the church. At one
extreme of the continuum there are the cultural musical forms that
inform the existence of these Black young people. At the other end
of the continuum, there is the worshipping life of the faith communities, to which these young people notionally belong. The latter
does not affirm nor provide space for the expressive qualities of the
former.

This failure to create meaningful links between the secular and
the overtly religious becomes yet another contributory factor for the
prevalence of a form of cultural dissonance within these churches.
The inability of these young people to 'feel at home'[71] in the church
contributes to a sense of estrangement. This, in turn, often leads to
a severing of the relationship between the church and the young
person, often effected in teenage years. This 'divorce' is a direct
result of the failure of the church to engage with pertinent issues
that are at play in the life experiences of these young people.

The continued music ministry of 'Soul and Spirit',[72] a Black
Methodist vocal trio, based at Moseley Road Methodist Church, in
Birmingham, has done much to create an African-centred approach
to music, that is reflective of Black popular culture and the
worshipping and ecclesiological traditions of historic-mainline
churches in Britain. This group is becoming increasingly well
known within Methodism and other circles. Their music ministry,
which includes many original songs, also involves the reinterpreting
of traditional hymns (usually through the addition of African-
centred rhythms). Their music has played an important role in
helping to develop a new example or model of Christian education
in the form of music within Methodism and other historic-mainline
churches.

The launch of Growing into Hope

Following the repeated piloting of the five sections of the draft
materials I had created, it was agreed that the impact of this work
should lead to a wider dissemination of this new curriculum. The
two books, products of this research project, were offered nationally,

courtesy of the ecumenical management committee in partnership with the Connexional Methodist Church and the Methodist Publishing House. The creation and final publication of *Growing into Hope* has been a crucial development. To the best of my knowledge, this publication is the first African-centred Christian education curriculum created in Europe. Its emergence has been the major tangible outcome of this study.

Conclusion

My desire, in the first instance, was to create a new example or model for the Christian education of Black children and young people in Britain. This was to be achieved by attempting to improve and change the practice of Christian education, as it was undertaken in a number of inner-city, historic-mainline churches in Birmingham. In short, I wanted to connect the teaching and learning of the Christian faith with the historic, sociocultural experiences of people of African descent. Of crucial importance, was the desire that this process should be fun!

In undertaking this task I was determined to act as a subjective insider. I make no pretence at being objective, neutral or dispassionate. My motivation to act was in part a reaction to my own individual journey towards liberation and selfhood.

The creation of *Growing into Hope* provided the catalyst for the tentative changes in the practice of Christian education in these churches. The element of cultural dissonance constrained many of the young people in the early part of the work. An element of cultural dissonance will remain prevalent within inner-city, historic-mainline churches as long as White, Eurocentric practices and traditions remain the norms that govern the life of these faith communities. While I can offer a number of examples where there has been a diminution in the pernicious effects of cultural dissonance, I realize that these are no more than fledgling changes against a backdrop of overarching White, Eurocentric normality. There is still much to do in this area, if we are to release the innate selfhood and expressions of faith of African and African-Caribbean people in historic-mainline churches.

It was refreshing to see a number of Black young people engaging with the African-centred Christian education materials. For many of these young people, it was the first opportunity they had received to link aspects of their Blackness with the Christian gospel. I believe that *Growing into Hope* provided these young people with an opportunity to envisage a more holistic perspective on the Christian faith. This new perspective for Christian education does not seek to dichotomize their existence. This approach attempts to surmount the traditional, historic divide between secular and religious, or White 'correctitude' and Black 'illegitimacy'. This duality has given rise to the divide between overt expressions of faith that are informed by White cultural norms and aesthetics, and African influenced, covert experiences, which are indicative of a more authentic, less mannered form of religious expression. Through the piloting of the many sections of material I began to witness the development of more unified, holistic expressions of faith and experience.

Through the development of improved and changed practice it became increasingly noticeable that a number of common factors were at play in these inner-city contexts. There was a growing awareness of the importance of Black cultural forms and expressions that are integral components of Black self-identity. A number of the youth and children's workers realized the necessity for worshipping communities to become settings where these cultural forms and expressions are the norm. In these contexts Black self-hood is affirmed and celebrated.

The use of an African-centred Christian education teaching and learning scheme gave rise to a plethora of new patterns of worship and learning in these inner-city churches. A number of these churches began to construct more participative and inclusive forms of worship that incorporated children and young people at the very heart of the faith community. These services attempted to celebrate and affirm the historic and more contemporary experiences and expressions of faith of African peoples. These acts of worship had an additional stated aim – the concurrent desire to liberate all marginalized people within the community of faith. Within these services Black children and young people were presented with opportunities to be proactive within worship. Similarly, many adults who had traditionally been silent and disaffected were given opportunities to become fuller members of the worshipping community. This development, which I have termed 'redefining the norm,' is applicable to the many diverse faith communities in Britain, where there exist structural imbalances in power and influence, with particular groups being marginalized.

The presence of younger Black leaders was crucial, as their ability to relate to Black young people was of paramount importance when using the Christian education materials. These leaders, all of whom were in their middle to late thirties, possessed an ability to work alongside Black youth. The abilities of such younger leaders were supplemented by an informed knowledge of Black popular cultures, and the importance of these expressive modes within the life experiences of Black youth. While every attempt was made to affirm and support the work of White, British junior church/Sunday school workers, this study clearly indicated that young Black leaders were more suited to this task. The dearth of Black male leaders was noted but, given the many specialist approaches that have been undertaken in this area, it was not within the scope of this study to address this issue directly.

Alongside the importance of younger Black leaders was the role undertaken by ordained clergy in these settings. The developments in improved and changed practice were most pronounced in those churches where the minister adopted an ideological position. The minister in these contexts sought to challenge the status quo, thereby creating appropriate spaces, in order that Black people might attempt to work out their liberation.

Given the relative importance of ministers in these inner-city contexts, it is vital that the training of such individuals takes account of the potentially oppressive nature of historic-mainline churches. Theological education needs to be informed by Black, Womanist and liberation theologies, transformative education and the more recent developments in practical theology. White, European ministers need to be aware of the historic and ongoing struggles for selfhood that is in evidence in the lives of people of African descent.

An informed awareness of these struggles will enable such individuals to be more effective in their ministry as it relates to contexts that are becoming increasingly African and African-Caribbean in complexion. Despite the effective work undertaken by a number of White, European ministers in these inner-city churches, one can only speculate as to the impact a minister of African descent might have exerted in one of these contexts. Clearly, there is a need for more Black ministers. The endemic racism inherent within candidating procedures and ministerial training within the historic-mainline churches is such that of the number of competent and credible Black people of faith who would make excellent ministers, only a small number feels able to place a tentative toe into the waters of ordained ministry. Within the different traditions of the historic-mainline churches in Britain, there is still a dearth of Black British-born people candidating for ordained ministry. From my interaction with Black young people in this study, this malaise has a long gestation period, with the varying levels of suspicion, uncertainty and a perceived lack of belonging going right back to adolescence.

This work, in many respects, is but the tip of hugely significant and increasingly important iceberg. The role of Black people of faith within historic-mainline churches is growing. Without our presence there would be very few churches in inner-city areas in Britain. Research by Brierley[73] has indicated the numerical ascendancy of Black people in metropolitan urban areas of Britain. If Black Christians (of whatever denomination) were to catch a cold or contract a virus that rendered us allergic to church, then most inner-city congregations in Britain would die. It is the Black presence that sustains much of inner-city church life in Britain today. Black cultures, experiences, spirituality and expressions of faith are revitalizing and challenging the historic definitions of what it means to be church.

Given the limitations of this work, this initiative can only be the start. *Growing into Hope*, the developmental and reflective work that gave rise to it and the analysis that has followed it are important first steps. I hope that this work will contribute to what will be a growing area in the theory and practice of a Black Christian education of liberation in Britain. May the journey from *Nobodies to Somebodies* continue.

Notes

Acknowledgements

1. The research project on which this study is based was given the title of the Birmingham Initiative. The Revd Christopher Hughes Smith, the then General Secretary of the Division of Education and Youth, having formerly been a minister and District Chairman in Birmingham, was aware of the deficiencies in the existing Christian education work sponsored by the Methodist Church amongst Black children and young people. The project ran from May 1995 to August 1999.

Chapter 1: 'Who Feels It, Knows It'

1. The term *youth* is used on a number of occasions. This term is used as a form of shorthand to denote *both* children and young people.
2. Womanist theology can be seen as a related branch of Black theology. It is an approach to theology that begins with the experience of Black women and women of colour. Womanist theology utilizes the experience of Black women to challenge the tripartite ills of racism, sexism and classism. This discipline is influenced by (Black) feminist thought. On occasions, Womanist theology has been inaccurately caricatured as *Black feminism*. Some important works by Womanist theologians include Katie G. Cannon *Black Womanist Ethics* (Atlanta, Georgia: Scholars Press, 1988), Emile M. Townes *Womanist Justice, Womanist Hope* (Atlanta, Georgia: Scholars Press, 1993), Jacquelyn Grant *White Women's Christ, Black Women's Jesus: Feminist Christology and Womanist Response* (Atlanta, Georgia: Scholars Press, 1989), Delores Williams *Sisters in the Wilderness: The Challenge of Womanist God-Talk* (Maryknoll, New York: Orbis Press, 1993).
3. See Paul Ballard and John Pritchard (eds.) *Practical Theology in Action* (London: SPCK, 1996) and Duncan B. Forrester *Truthful Action: Explorations in Practical Theology* (Edinburgh: T & T Clark, 2000).
4. See Jeff Astley and Colin Crowder 'Theological Perspectives on Christian Education: An Overview' in Jeff Astley, Leslie J. Francis and Colin Crowder (eds.) *Theological Perspectives on Christian Formation: A Reader on Theology and Christian Education* (Grand Rapids, Michigan: W. B. Eerdmans, 1996), pp. x–xix.
5. See Robert Beckford *Jesus is Dread: Black Theology and Black Culture in Britain* (London: Darton, Longman and Todd, 1998), *Dread and Pentecostal: A*

Political Theology for the Black Church in Britain (London: SPCK, 2000) and *God of the Rahtid* (London: Darton, Longman and Todd, 2001). See also *Black Theology in Britain: A Journal of Contextual Praxis* (Sheffield: Sheffield Academic Press) (This journal was renamed *Black Theology: An International Journal* from November 2002. It is now published by Continuum.); Paul Grant and Raj Patel (eds.) *A Time to Speak* (Birmingham: A joint publication of Racial Justice and the Black Theology Working Group, 1990), and *A Time to Act*: *Kairos 1992* (Birmingham: A joint publication of 'Racial Justice' and the 'Black Theology Working Group', 1992); Joe Aldred *Preaching with Power* (London: Cassells, 1998), *Sisters with Power* (London: Continuum, 2000) and *Praying with Power* (London: Continuum, 2000); Anthony G. Reddie, *Faith, Stories and the Experience of Black Elders: Singing the Lord's Song in a Strange Land* (London: Jessica Kingsley, 2001).

6. By historic-mainline, I mean those established denominations of the Protestant tradition which account for the greater majority of the population that can be described and identified as church attendees and practising Christians. The churches in question are Methodist, Anglican, Baptist and United Reformed.

7. Joyce Bailey '*Fashion Me a People*: A New Ecumenical Caribbean Curriculum', *Religious Education* Vol. 75, No. 5, Sept.–Oct. 1980, p. 580.

8. Robert Beckford, 1998, pp. 42–58.

9. John Sutcliffe (ed.) *Tuesday's Child: A Reader for Christian Educators* (Birmingham: Christian Education Publishers, 2001).

10. Walter Rodney *The Groundings with my Brothers* (New York: Grove Books, 1986), pp. 32–3.

11. Caryl Phillips mentions the psychological and emotional dissonance in the individual experience of Black youth, when commenting upon his own formative development in his book *The European Tribe* (London: Faber and Faber, 1987), pp. 1–9.

12. Vincent Harding 'Black Power and the American Christ' in Gayraud S. Wilmore and James H. Cone (eds.) *Black Theology: A Documentary History, 1966–1979* (New York: Orbis Books, 1979), p. 37.

13. Jeff Astley, Leslie J. Francis and Colin Crowder (eds.) *Theological Perspectives on Christian Formation* (Grand Rapids, Michigan: Eerdmans, 1996), p. x.

14. Jeff Astley *The Philosophy of Christian Religious Education* (Birmingham, Alabama: Religious Education Press, 1994).

15. Ian Duffield 'Blacks in Britain: History and the Historians', *History Today* Vol. 31, Sept. 1981, p. 34.

16. Peter Fryer *Staying Power: The History of Black People in Britain* (London: Pluto Press, 1984), p. 10.

17. See Gretchen Gerzina *Black England: Life Before Emancipation* (London: John Murray, 1995) and Ron Ramdin *Reimaging Britain: 500 years of Black and Asian History* (London: Pluto Press, 1999).

18. Ceri Peach *West Indian Migration to Britain: A Social Geography* (London: Oxford University Press, 1968), p. 82.

19. Ceri Peach 'Black-Caribbean: Class, Gender and Geography' in Ceri Peach (ed.) *Ethnicity in the 1991 Census: Vol. 2 (The Ethnic Minority Populations of Great Britain)* (London: HMSO, 1996), p. 27.

20. R. Balarajan and L. Bulusu 'Mortality among Immigrants in England and Wales, 1973–1983' in M. Britton (ed.) *Mortality and Geography (OPCS Series DS No.9)* (London: HMSO, 1990), pp. 135–50.

21. Heather Walton *A Tree God Planted: Black People in British Methodism* (London: Ethnic Minorities In Methodism Working Group, The Methodist Church, 1984).

22. Renate Wilkinson 'A Chance to Change' in *Inheritors Together: Black People in the Church of England* (London: Race, Pluralism and Community Group, Board for Social Responsibility, The Church of England, 1985), p. 20.

23. Ceri Peach 'Black-Caribbean: Class, Gender and Geography', p. 27.

24. Tony Holden *People, Churches and Multi-Racial Projects* (London: The Division of Social Responsibility, The Methodist Church, 1985), p. 29.

25. Clarice T. Nelson 'The Churches, Racism and the Inner-cities' in Paul Grant and Raj Patel (eds.) *A Time to Speak* (Birmingham: A joint publication of Racial Justice and the Black Theology Working Group, 1990), p. 4.

26. Clarice T. Nelson 'The Churches, Racism and the Inner-cities', p. 4.

27. Lord Scarman 'Inner City Problems', *Hansard*, Vol. 484, Feb. 1987, pp. 13–24.

28. John Wilkinson 'Inheritors Together' in *Inheritors Together: Black People in the Church of England* (London: Race, Pluralism and Community Group, Board for Social Responsibility, The Church of England, 1985), p. 16.

29. See David Sheppard *Bias to the Poor* (London: Hodder and Stoughton, 1983); *Faith in the City: Archbishop's Commission on Urban Priority Areas* (London: Church House Publications, 1985); *Anglicans and Racism* (London: Board for Social Responsibility, Church House Publications, 1986); *Faithful and Equal:* The Report Adopted at the Portsmouth Methodist Conference (The Methodist Church 1987); *Rainbow Gospel* (London: The British Council of Churches, 1988); *Seeds of Hope: Report of a Survey on Combating Racism in the Dioceses of the Church of England* (London: Church House Publications, 1991); *The Passing Winter: A Sequel to Seeds of Hope* (London: Church House Publications, 1996).

30. Elton Lewis 'Redemption Song' in Paul Grant and Raj Patel (eds.), 1992, pp. 8–18.

31. Clarice T. Nelson and Sybil Phoenix in Paul Grant and Raj Patel (eds.), 1992, pp. 19–23.

32. Gayraud S. Wilmore *Black Religion and Black Radicalism* (New York: Orbis Books, 1983), pp. 1–28.

33. Gayraud S. Wilmore, 1983, pp. 5–9.

34. Gayraud S. Wilmore, 1983, pp. 12–28.

35. Clarice T. Nelson 'The Churches, Racism and the Inner-cities', p. 9.

36. Odida T. Quamina *All Things Considered: Can We Live Together?* (Toronto: Exile Editions, 1996), pp. 201–12.

37. Paul Hartman and Charles Hubbard *Racism and the Mass Media* (London: Davis Poynter, 1974), p. 146.

38. Erik H. Erikson *Identity: Youth and Crisis* (New York: W.W. Norton, 1984), p. 16.

39. Erik H. Erikson, 1984, p. 17.

40. Erik H. Erikson, 1984, p. 21.

41. Erik H. Erikson, 1984, pp. 208–12.

42. Sigmund Freud 'Address to the Society of B'Nai B'rith 1926' in *Freud's Works* Standard Edition, Vol. 20 (London: Hogarth Press. 1959), p. 273.

43. Henry James *The Letters of Henry James Vol.1* (Boston: The Atlantic Monthly Press, 1920), p. 199.

44. James Walvin *Black Ivory: A History of British Slavery* (London: Fontana Press, 1993), pp. 301–36.

45. David Northrup (ed.) *The Atlantic Slave Trade* (Lexington, MA: D.C. Heath Co., 1994), pp. 12–35. See also Carter G. Woodson *The Miseducation of the Negro* [first published in 1933] (Trenton, New Jersey: Africa World Press, 1990), pp. xii–xiii.

46. Robert Nesta Marley 'Redemption Song', from the album *Uprising*. © Bob Marley Music, Island Records, 1980.

47. Frantz Fanon *The Wretched of the Earth* (New York: Grove Books, 1984), p. 52.

48. Erik H. Erikson, 1984, p. 59.

49. W. E. B. Dubois *The Souls of Black Folk* (New York: Bantam. 1989), p. 3.

50. W. E. B. Dubois, 1989, p. 3.

51. Ron Ramdin *Reimaging Britain* (London: Pluto Press, 1999), pp. 333–6.

52. Winston James 'Migration, Racism and Identity' in Winston James and Clive Harris (eds.) *Inside Babylon* (London: Verso, 1993), p. 9.

53. G. Lewis 'Race Relations in Britain: A View from the Caribbean' *Race Today* Vol. 1, No.3 (1969), p. 9. See also Barbara Bush *Slave Women in Caribbean Society: 1650–1838* (Kingston, Jamaica: Heinemann, 1990).

54. A child of a 'negro' mother and a 'negro' father.

55. A child of a mother who is one fifth Black and a White man. See B. Higman *Slave Populations and Economy in Jamaica: 1807–1834* (London: Cambridge University Press, 1976), p. 139.

56. Winston James, 1993, p. 234.

57. Winston James, 1993, p. 234.

58. Winston James, 1993, p. 33.

59. Caryl Phillips *The European Tribe* (London: Faber and Faber, 1987).

60. Caryl Phillips, 1987, p. 2.

61. See Vanessa Howard 'A Report on Afro-Caribbean Christianity in Britain', Community Religions Project, University of Leeds, 1987, p. 23. According to Howard, 52% of the African Caribbean population in the United Kingdom are British born.

62. Paul Gilroy *Small Acts* (London: Serpents Tail, 1993), pp. 49–62.

63. This can be seen in the fact that prior to the independence of the former colonies of the British empire, many of the Black migrants who came to Britain, during the mass migration of the post Second World War era (see the earlier section entitled 'The social, historical and political background' in this chapter), came as British subjects, complete with British passports. While there existed a great deal of political and cultural pressure for them to conform to a centrally defined notion of being British, there was no denying their right to apply that phrase to themselves.

64. For a useful overview of this phenomenon see A. Sivanandan *Communities of Resistance* (London: Verso, 1990).

65. See Kwesi Owusu (ed.) *Black British Culture and Society: A Text Reader* (London: Routledge, 2000), pp. 1–18.

66. Ernest E. Cashmore and Barry Troyna (eds.) *Black Youth in Crisis* (London: Allen and Unwin, 1982), p. 17.

67. Ernest E. Cashmore and Barry Troyna (eds.), 1982, p. 26.

68. William David Spencer *Dread Jesus* (London: SPCK, 1999).

69. Ken Pryce *Endless Pressure* (Bristol: Bristol Classical Press, 1979), p. 145.

70. Robert Beckford, 1998, pp. 115–29.

71. See Barry Chevannes (ed.) *Rastafari and other African Caribbean Worldviews* (London: Macmillan Press, 1998).

72. William David Spencer, 1999, pp. 117–21.

73. A helpful source for further analysis on this matter is *The Alarm* magazine (Alarm Publications, London). This publication is a good example of an Afrocentric publication that attempts to construct a coherent African hermeneutic on issues as diverse as politics, history, economics and sociology.

74. For a useful insight into the phenomenon of the Nation of Islam, see Mattias Gardell *Countdown to Armageddon: Louis Farrakhan and the Nation of Islam* (London: C. Hurst, 1996), pp. 1–30. Gardell identifies the Nation of Islam as part of the wider struggle of Black people to gain a positive identity. See also Martha Lee *The Nation of Islam: An American Millenarian Movement* (New York: Syracuse University Press, 1988), pp. 1–115. See also Aminah B. McCloud *African American Islam* (New York: Routledge, 1995), pp. 27–52.

75. Paul Gilroy, 1993, p. 124. This term refers to a commonly perceived trait within Afrocentricity, which relates to 'essential' characteristics, factors and outlook, beliefs and philosophies that can be seen as being an indispensable part of being Black. Deviation or divergence from these 'norms' can be interpreted as a diminution of the Black African heritage. Critics of 'essentialism' assert that this trait within Afrocentricity attempts to impose a rigid straitjacket of homogeneity and conformity across Black cultural life, and refuses to acknowledge the pluralistic nature of Black life across the whole world.

76. Paul Gilroy, 1993, p. 128.

77. Paul Gilroy, 1993, p. 61.

78. Tony Sewell *Black Masculinities and Schooling* (Stoke-on-Trent: Trentham Books, 1997), p. 163.

79. Tony Sewell, 1997, p. 163.

80. Les Back *Youth, Racism and Ethnicity in South London* (London: Unpublished Ph.D thesis, University of London, 1992), p. 52.

81. Paul Gilroy, 1993, p. 141.

82. This metaphor of jazz music was first used in Anthony G. Reddie *Faith, Stories and Experience of Black Elders: Singing The Lord's Song in a Strange Land* (London: Jessica Kingsley, 2001), pp. 92–4.

83. See Geoffrey C. Ward and Ken Burns *Jazz: A History of America's music* (London: Pimlico, 2001), pp. 344–57).

84. See 'The Impact of The Oral Tradition Conversations in Black Children' in Anthony G. Reddie *Faith, Stories and Experience of Black Elders: Singing the Lord's Song in a Strange Land* (London: Jessica Kingsley, 2001).

85. Molefi Kete Asante 'Afrocentricity and Culture' in Molefi Kete Asante and Kariamu Welsh Asante (eds.) *African Culture: The Rhythms of Unity* (New Jersey: First Africa World Press, 1990), p. 4.

86. Gayraud S. Wilmore 'Black Theology and the Black Church: Introduction' in Gayraud S. Wilmore and James H. Cone (eds.) *Black Theology: A Documentary History, 1966–1979* (New York: Orbis, 1979), p. 243.

87. A. V. Kelly *Knowledge and Programme Planning* (San Francisco: Harper and Row, 1986), p. 158.

88. Anne Hope and Sally Timmel *Training for Transformation Vol. 4* (Southampton: Intermediate Publications, 1999), pp. 186–209.

89. Cheikh Anta Diop *The African Origin of Civilization* (Chicago: Lawrence Hill Books, 1974).

90. Molefi Kete Asante *Afrocentricity* (Trenton, New Jersey: African World Press, 1988), p. 61.

91. Molefi Kete Asante and Kariamu Welsh Asante (eds.), 1990, p. 11.

92. Molefi Kete Asante and Kariamu Welsh Asante (eds.), 1990, p. 6.

93. W. E. B. Dubois 'The African Roots of War' (1915) in Meyer Wenberg (ed.) *W. E. B. Dubois: A Reader* (New York: Harper and Row, 1970), pp. 360–71.

94. Maulana Karenga *Introduction to Black Studies* (Inglewood, California: Kawaida, 1982), p. 36.

95. Paul Gilroy 'It's a Family Affair' in Gina Dent (ed.) *Black Popular Culture* (Seattle: Bay Press, 1992), p. 306.

96. Stuart Hall 'Old and New Identities, Old and New Ethnicities' in A. D. King (ed.) *Culture Globalization and the World System* (Hampshire: Macmillan, 1991), p. 57.

97. Paul Gilroy 'It's a Family Affair', in Gina Dent (ed.), 1992, pp. 306–7 and Tony Sewell, 1997, p. 163.

98. Robert Beckford, 1998, p. 15.

Chapter 2: 'Pioneers Along the Way'

1. The work of The Commission for Black Sunday School Development in association with Target Timothy, in South Africa and the wider liberation struggle of Southern Africa is a noted exception. See my later references to the work of Target Timothy and *Umalusi* in the early 1980s.

2. James H. Cone *God of the Oppressed* (San Francisco: Harper, 1975) and James H. Cone *A Black Theology of Liberation* (New York: Orbis, 1986). See also Dwight N. Hopkins *(Introducing) Black Theology of Liberation* (Maryknoll, New York: Orbis, 1999).

3. Olivia Pearl Stokes 'Black Theology: A Challenge to Religious Education' in Norma H. Thompson (ed.) *Religious Education and Theology* (Birmingham, Alabama: Religious Education Press, 1982), p. 71.

4. James H. Cone *Black Theology and Black Power* (New York: Orbis, 1986), pp. 62–90.

5. James H. Cone, 1975, p. 18.

6. James H. Cone, 1986, p. 1.

7. James H. Cone, 1986, p. 5.

8. Olivia Pearl Stokes, 1982, p. 71.

9. Olivia Pearl Stokes, 1982, pp. 86–8.

10. *Spectrum* No. 47, Jul/Aug 1971.

11. Enoch H. Oglesby 'Ethical and Educational Implications of Black Theology in America', *Religious Education* Vol. 69, No. 4, Jan.–Feb. 1974, p. 406.

12. Enoch H. Oglesby, 1974, p. 411.

13. *Religious Education* Vol. 64, No. 6, Nov.–Dec. 1969.

14. Joseph A. Johnson Jnr 'The Imperative of Beyondness', *Religious Education* Vol. 64, No. 6, Nov.–Dec. 1969, p. 439.

15. Joseph A. Johnson Jnr, 1969, p. 439.

16. C. D. Coleman 'Agenda for the Black Church', Andrew White 'Why the Church should Evangelise Black Youth', Jeffrey N. Stinehelfer 'Dig This: The Revealing of Jesus Christ', Allen J. Moore 'An Educational Approach to Renewal in Local Churches', *Religious Education* Vol. 64, No. 6, Nov.–Dec. 1969.

17. Collen Birchett 'A History of Religious Education in the Black Church' in Donald B. Rogers (ed.) *Urban Church Education* (Birmingham, Alabama: Religious Education Press, 1989), Chapter 7.

18. Collen Birchett, 1989, p. 76.

19. Collen Birchett, 1989, p. 79.

20. An example of this can be seen in Robert Beckford's book *Dread and Pentecostal: A Political Theology for the Black Church in Britain* (London: SPCK, 2000).

21. For further details see E. Franklin Frazier *The Negro Church in America* (New York: Shocken Books, 1964), and C. Eric Lincoln *The Black Church in the African American Experience* (Durham, N.Y.: Duke University Press, 1990). See also an excellent new book by Anne H. Pinn and Anthony B. Pinn *The History of the Black Church* (Minneapolis: Fortress Press, 2002).

22. Andrew White 'Why Should the Church Evangelise Black Youth?', *Religious Education* Vol. 64, No. 6, Nov.–Dec. 1969, pp. 447–8.

23. Lonzy Edwards 'Religious Education by Blacks during Reconstruction', *Religious Education* Vol. 69, No. 4, Jan.–Feb. 1974, pp. 412–13.

24. Calvin E. Bruce 'Refocusing Black Religious Education: 3 Imperatives', *Religious Education* Vol. 69, No. 4, Jan.–Feb. 1974, p. 432.

25. Lawrence N. Jones 'Hope For Mankind: Insights From Black Religious History in the United States of America', *Journal of Religious Thought* Vol. 34, No. 2, Fall–Winter 1978, pp. 64–5.

26. Lawrence N. Jones, 1978, p. 62.

27. Bonita Pope Curry 'The Role of the Church in the Educational Development of Black Children' in Lee N. June (ed.) *The Black Family* (Grand Rapids, Michigan: Zondervan Publishing House, 1991), p. 116.

28. C. D. Coleman 'Agenda for the Black Church', *Religious Education* Vol. 64, No. 6, Nov.–Dec. 1969, p. 441.

29. C. D. Coleman, 1969, p. 442.

30. James H. Harris 'Black Church and Black Theology: Theory and Practice' in James H. Cone and Gayraud S. Wilmore (eds.) *Black Theology: A Documentary History Vol. 2, 1980–1992* (Maryknoll, New York: Orbis, 1993), pp. 85–97.

31. Riggins Earl Jnr *To You Who Teach in the Black Church* (Nashville: National Baptist Publishing Board, 1972), p. 77.

32. William A. Jones Jnr 'Confronting the System' in Gayraud S. Wilmore (ed.) *African American Religious Studies: An Interdisciplinary Anthology* (Durham and London: Duke University Press, 1989), pp. 429–57.

33. Mary A. Love 'Musings on Sunday School in the Black Community' in D. Campbell Wyckoff (ed.) *Renewing the Sunday School and the CCD* (Birmingham, Alabama: Religious Education Press, 1986), p. 155.

34. Mary A. Love, 1986, pp. 160–1.

35. R. Johnson 'The Black Church and the Sunday School Movement', *The Church School Herald-Journal* Vol. 66, No. 2, Dec., Jan., Feb. 1980–1, p. 11.

36. Harold Dean Trulear 'African American Religious Education' in Barbara Wilkerson *Multi-Cultural Religious Education* (Birmingham, Alabama: Religious Education Press, 1997), p. 166.

37. See Robinson Milwood *Liberation and Mission* (London: African Caribbean Education Resource Centre [ACER], 1997) and John Wilkinson *The Church in Black and White: The Black Tradition in Mainstream Churches in England* (Edinburgh: Saint Andrew, 1993) as two examples of recent literature that attempt to explicate a Black British theology from within the historic-mainline tradition.

38. This theme will be discussed in Chapter 4. See 'Redefining the norm', p. 132.

39. Grant Shockley was born in Philadelphia in 1919 where he grew up attending segregated schools. He was raised in the Methodist Church and graduated from Lincoln University, a Black college in Pennsylvania. Following a further period of study, he graduated also from Drew Theological Seminary. Shockley was ordained

into the ministry of the United Methodist Church. He was appointed to serve the Janes Methodist Church in Brooklyn, the first Black congregation in the New York Conference. Further study led to his completing an Ed. D. at Teachers College, Columbia University. One of his earliest teaching appointments was at Clark University. Aside from his academic teaching career, he served as the Secretary of Missionary Education for the Board of Missions of the United Methodist Church, a job that took him all over the world at the height of the Civil Rights Movement. Later teaching appointments included Garrett Theological Seminary in Evanston, Illinois, and the Candler School of Theology in Atlanta (the first African-American on both faculties). He then became president of the Interdenominational Theological Center in Atlanta. Following his stint in Atlanta, Shockley became president of Philander Smith College in Arkansas. Shockley moved from Philander to join the Duke Divinity School faculty from where he retired. After retirement he became an emeritus professor and taught at Candler and Clark again. Shockley wrote many articles on Christian religious education in which he took seriously the Black religious experience in general, commenting in particular on the Black Methodist experience. Grant Shockley died in 1996.

40. Important articles by Grant S. Shockley include 'Christian Education and the Black Church: A Contextual Approach', *Journal of the Interdenominational Theological Center* Spring 1975, pp. 75–8; 'From Emancipation to Transformation to Consummation: a Black Perspective' in Marlene Mayr (ed.) *Does the Church Really Want Religious Education?* (Birmingham, Alabama: Religious Education Press, 1988), pp. 221–48; 'Liberation Theology, Black Theology, and Religious Education' in M. Taylor (ed.) *Foundations for Christian Education* (Nashville, Tenn.: Abingdon Press, 1976), pp. 80–95; 'Black Liberation, Christian Education and Black Social Indicators', *Duke Divinity School Review* No. 40, Spring 1975, pp. 109–25.

41. Grant S. Shockley 'Black Pastoral Leadership in Religious Education'. Robert L. Browning (ed.) *The Pastor as Religious Educator* (Birmingham, Alabama: Religious Education Press, 1987), p. 195.

42. Grant S. Shockley 'Black Theology and Religious Education' in Randolph Crump Miller (ed.) *Theologies of Religious Education* (Birmingham, Alabama: Religious Education Press, 1995), p. 323.

43. Grant S. Shockley, 1995, p. 315.

44. Grant S. Shockley, 1995, p. 321.

45. Grant S. Shockley 'Christian Education and the Black Religious Experience' in Charles R. Foster *Ethnicity in the Education of the Church* (Nashville, Tenn.: Conference Papers/Scarritt Graduate School, Scarritt Press, 1987), pp. 31–5.

46. Grant S. Shockley, 1987, pp. 33–4.

47. Grant S. Shockley, 1987, pp. 38–40.

48. Grant S. Shockley 'From Emancipation to Transformation to Consummation: A Black Perspective' in Marlene Mayr (ed.) *Does the Church Really Want Religious Education?* (Birmingham, Alabama: Religious Education Press, 1988), pp. 244–6.

49. See Charles R. Foster and Grant S. Shockley (eds.) *Working with Black Youth* (Nashville, Tenn.: Abingdon Press, 1989).

50. Charles R. Foster 'Faith Community as a Guiding Image for Christian Education' in Jack L. Seymour and Donald E. Miller (eds.) *Contemporary Approaches to Christian Education* (Nashville: Abingdon Press, 1982), p. 64.

51. Charles R. Foster 'Double Messages: Ethnocentrism in Church Education', *Religious Education* Vol. 82, No. 3, Summer 1987, p. 467.

52. Charles R. Foster, 1987, p. 467.

53. Charles R. Foster 'Imperialism in the Religious Education of Cultural Minorities', *Religious Education* Vol. 86, No. 1, Winter 1991, pp. 153–4.

54. Charles R. Foster, 1991, p. 155.

55. Charles R. Foster 'The Pastor: Agent of Vision in the Education of a Community of Faith' in Robert L. Browning (ed.) *The Pastor as Religious Educator* (Birmingham, Alabama: Religious Education Press, 1987), p. 23.

56. Harold William Burgess *An Invitation to Religious Education* (Mishawaka, Indiana: Religious Education Press, 1975), p. 21.

57. See the work of George Albert Coe, who is sometimes identified as being the father of the liberal approach, and more recently, the work of James Michael Lee. Lee is credited with being one of the leading apologists for the social scientific, non-transcendental approach to religious education.

58. James Michael Lee 'Religious Education and Theology' in Jeff Astley, Leslie J. Francis and Colin Crowder (eds.) *Theological Perspectives on Christian Formation* (Grand Rapids, Michigan: W.B. Eerdmans, 1996), pp. 43–66.

59. Milton E. Owens 'Black Awareness: Re-established Dignity', *Spectrum* Vol. 49, Spring 1973, p. 16.

60. Joseph V. Crockett *Teaching Scripture: From an African American Perspective* (Nashville, Tenn.: Discipleship Resources, 1989).

61. Milton E. Owens, 1973, p. 17.

62. Cain Hope Felder 'The Bible – Re-Contextualisation and the Black Religious Experience' in Gayraud S. Wilmore (ed.) *African American Religious Studies: An Interdisciplinary Anthology* (Durham and London: Duke University Press, 1989), pp. 156–68.

63. Cain Hope Felder, 1989, p. 168.

64. Keith A. Chism *A Christian Education for the African American Community* (Nashville, Tenn.: Discipleship Resources, 1995), p. 36.

65. See R. S. Sugirtharajah *Voices From the Margins* (New York/London: Orbis/SPCK, 1991), *The Post Colonial Bible* (Sheffield: Sheffield Academic Press, 1998) and *The Bible and the Third World* (Cambridge: Cambridge University Press, 2001).

66. Janice Hale-Benson *Black Children: Their Roots, Cultures and Learning Styles* (Baltimore: The Johns Hopkins University Press, 1986), pp. 4–5.

67. Janice Hale-Benson, 1986, pp. 21–4.

68. Rosalie Cohen 'Conceptual Styles, Culture Conflict and Non-verbal Tests of Intelligence', *American Anthropologist* No. 71, pp. 828–56.

69. Janice Hale-Benson, 1986, pp. 30–42.

70. Janice Hale-Benson, 1986, p. 38.

71. Janice Hale *Unbank the Fire: Visions for the Education of African American Children* (Baltimore: The Johns Hopkins University Press, 1994), pp. 7–10. See also Anthony G. Reddie *Faith, Stories and Experience of Black Elders: Singing The Lord's Song in a Strange Land* (London: Jessica Kingsley, 2001) for a more detailed exploration of the oral traditions of Black people.

72. Janice Hale, 1994, pp. 7–10.

73. Janice Hale, 1994, pp. 79–84.

74. Earl Beckles 'The Language Needs of Children of West Indian Origin', *Multicultural Teaching* Vol. 8, No. 2, Spring 1990, pp. 38–41.

75. Janice Hale 'The Transmission of Cultural Values to Young African American Children', *Journal Of Young Children* Vol. 46, Issue 6, 1990, p. 7.

76. Janice Hale, 1990, pp. 9–13.

77. Janice Hale-Benson 'Visions for Children: Educating Black Children in the Context of their Culture' in Kofi Lomotey (ed.) *Going to School: The African-American Experience* (New York: State University of New York Press, 1990), pp. 210–17.

78. Michael Ross *Building Positive Images in African American Males Through the Sunday School from a Black Perspective* (Unpublished D. Min. thesis, United Theological Seminary, 1993).

79. Helen A. Archibald 'Notes on the Culture of the Urban Negro Child', *Religious Education* Vol. 62, No. 4, July–Aug. 1967, p. 324.

80. Helen A. Archibald, 1967, p. 325.

81. Andrew White, 1969, pp. 447–8.

82. Andrew White, 1969, p. 449.

83. Nelson E. Copeland Jnr. *The Heroic Revolution: A New Agenda for Urban Youth Work* (Nashville, Tenn.: The James C. Winston Publishing Company, 1995), pp. 27–31.

84. Nelson E. Copeland Jnr, 1995, pp. 83–5.

85. Nelson E. Copeland Jnr, 1995, p. 85.

86. Na'im Akbar *Chains and Images of Psychological Slavery* (Jersey City: New Mind Publications, 1984), pp. 20–3.

87. Useni Eugene Perkins *Harvesting New Generations: The Positive Development of Black Youth* (Chicago: Third World Press, 1986), pp. 3–7.

88. Useni Eugene Perkins, 1986, pp. 79–115.

89. Michael A. Clarke *Reclaiming The Black Experience in the Anglican Church in Barbados: A Study Amongst a Group of Young Anglicans* (Unpublished D. Min. thesis, Toronto School of Theology, Trinity College, Ontario, 1995).

90. Michael A. Clarke, 1995, pp. 85–100.

91. George L. Champion *Christian Education for the African American Church* (Riviera Beach, Florida: Port Printing Company, 1990), pp. 18–49.

92. George L. Champion, 1990, pp. 183–97.

93. James Michael Lee, 1996, pp. 47–8.

94. See Grant S. Shockley, 1987.

95. Jawanza Kunjufu *Developing Positive Self-Images and Discipline in Black Children* (Chicago: African American Images, 1984), pp. 2–14.

96. Jawanza Kunjufu *Motivating and Preparing Black Youth to Work* (Chicago: African American Images, 1986), pp. 22–4.

97. Jawanza Kunjufu *Critical Issues in Educating African American Youth* (Chicago: African American Images, 1989).

98. Jawanza Kunjufu, 1989, p. 23.

99. See Jawanza Kunjufu *Countering the Conspiracy to Destroy Black Boys*, 3 volumes (Chicago: African American Images, 1982–1990).

100. Jawanza Kunjufu *Countering the Conspiracy to Destroy Black Boys* Vol. 3, 1990, p. 31.

101. Mentoring in this context is the pairing of an older adult with a younger person from (usually) the same community or culture. The former will be an individual with whom the younger respondent can identify, and from whom they can gain invaluable assistance in understanding some of the complex issues at play in the process of developing a positive Black identity. The whole issue of mentoring and 'rites of passage' is becoming increasingly prevalent within the literature pertaining to Black young people of African descent. See Jawanza Kunjufu *Developing Positive Self-Images and Discipline in Black Children* (Chicago: African American Images, 1984), and *Motivating and Preparing Black Youth to Work* (Chicago: African American Images, 1986) and Aminifu R. Harvey and Antionatte A. Coleman 'An Afrocentric Program for African American Males in the Juvenile Justice System' in Sondra Jackson and Sheryl Brissett-Chapman (eds.) *Child Welfare: The Journal of Policy, Practice and Program* Vol. 76, No. 1, Jan.–Feb. 1997, pp. 197–211.

102. Reva Klein 'Escape Route from the Fire of Alienation', *Times Educational Supplement* No. 4102, Section 2, 10 Feb. 1995, p. 6.

103. Gloria Morgan 'An Investigation into the Achievement of African Caribbean pupils', *Multicultural Teaching* Vol. 14, No. 2, Spring 1996, p. 38.

104. Mike Vance 'Changing Expectations: Working with Disaffected African Caribbean Boys', *Multicultural Teaching* Vol. 15, No. 2, Spring 1997, p. 32.

105. Tony Sewell *Black Masculinities and Schooling* (Stoke-on-Trent: Trentham Books, 1997), pp. 216–20.

106. David Gillborn *'Race', Ethnicity and Education: Teaching and Learning in Multi-Ethnic Schools* (London: Allen and Unwin, 1990).

107. Mairtin Mac an Ghaill, *The Making of Men, Masculinities, Sexualities and Schooling* (Buckingham: Open University Press, 1994).

108. Jim Cummins 'Negotiating Identities in the Classroom and Society', *Multicultural Teaching* Vol. 15, No. 1, Autumn 1996, p. 7.

109. Edward Coard *How the West Indian Child is made Educationally Subnormal in the British School System: The Scandal of the Black Child in Britain* (London: New Beacon Books, 1971).

110. George S. Richards 'Supplementary Schools – Their Service to Education', *Multicultural Teaching* Vol. 14, No. 1, Autumn 1995, p. 36.

111. George S. Richards, 1995, pp. 36–9.

112. Corrine Julius 'Trainers Score in Extra Time', *Times Educational Supplement* No. 4263, 13 March 1998, p. 16.

113. Reva Klein 'The Pile 'em High Club', *Times Educational Supplement* No. 4208, Section 2, 21 Feb. 1997, pp. 4–5.

114. Reva Klein 'Myth and Reality of the Race factor', *Times Educational Supplement* No. 4117, 26 May 1995, p. 10.

115. Reva Klein 'Race Inequality – as bad as ever', *Times Educational Supplement* No. 4184, 6 Sept. 1996, p. 13.

116. Reva Klein 'The Lost Generation', *Times Educational Supplement* No. 4165, 26 April 1996, pp. 3–4.

117. Elizabeth Rasekoala 'Ethnic Minorities and Achievement: The Fog Clears', *Multicultural Teaching* Vol. 15, No. 2, Spring 1997, pp. 24–8.

118. In more recent times the African Caribbean Evangelical Alliance (ACEA) has set up its Children's and Youth Commission (CandY) to look at the broader task of nurturing and supporting Black children and young people within the context of Christian faith. The commission is headed by Carver Anderson, National Director of Youth and Christian Education, New Testament Church of God. ACEA hosted a major conference entitled 'Serve Them Right' (29 September 2001), which sought to address many of the issues with which 'Drinking from our own Wells' had conspicuously failed to engage. Although 'Serve Them Right' offered a more realistic and credible Biblical hermeneutic and pedagogy for engaging with Black youth, its effectiveness, nevertheless, was limited by many of the fault-lines I have identified with 'Drinking from our own Wells'.

119. See Vol. 2 of *Growing into Hope: Liberation and Change* (Peterborough: Methodist Publishing House, 1998), p. 116.

120. Gayraud S. Wilmore *Black Religion and Black Radicalism* (New York: Orbis, 1983), pp. 1–28.

121. Albert Rabateau *Slave Religion* (London: Oxford University Press, 1978), pp. 44–150.

122. See R. S. Sugirtharajah *The Bible and the Third World* (Cambridge: Cambridge University Press, 2001).

123. *Echoes*: Teacher's Commentary (Colorado Springs: D. C. Cook Communication Ministries, 1996), p. 3.

124. *Umalusi: Christian Education for Children* (Cape Town: The Commission for Black Sunday School Development in Association with Target Timothy, 1983).

125. See Robert E. Hood *Must God Remain Greek?* (Minneapolis: Fortress Press, 1990). Specifically within the context of the continent of Africa I would recommend Paul John Issak *Religion and Society: A Namibian Perspective* (Windhoek, Namibia: Out of Africa Publishers, 1997).

126. Joyce Bailey '*Fashion Me a People*: A New Ecumenical Caribbean Curriculum', *Religious Education* Vol. 75, No. 5, Sept.–Oct. 1980, pp. 577–91.

127. Joyce Bailey, 1980, pp. 578–80.

128. *Fashion Me a People* (Jamaica: Caribbean Conference of Churches, 1985).

Chapter 3: Bringing the Thing to Life

1. Womanist theology can be seen as a related branch of Black theology. It is an approach to theology that begins with the experience of Black women and women of colour. Womanist theology utilizes the experience of Black women to challenge the tripartite ills of racism, sexism and classism. This discipline is influenced by (Black) feminist thought. On occasions, Womanist theology has been inaccurately caricatured as *Black feminism*. Some important works by Womanist theologians include Katie G. Cannon *Black Womanist Ethics* (Atlanta, Georgia: Scholars Press, 1988), Emile M. Townes *Womanist Justice, Womanist Hope* (Atlanta, Georgia: Scholars Press, 1993), Jacquelyn Grant *White Women's Christ, Black Women's Jesus: Feminist Christology and Womanist Response* (Atlanta, Georgia: Scholars Press, 1989) and Delores Williams *Sisters in the Wilderness: The Challenge of Womanist God-Talk* (Maryknoll, New York: Orbis Press, 1993).

2. The draft curriculum was written in five parts. *Advent* (first issued in Dec. 1995. Material for 4 weeks), *Pentecost* (May 1996. Material for 2 weeks), *Harvest* (October 1996. Material for 1 week), *Covenant* (Jan. 1997. Material for 1 week) and *Lent and Easter* (March/April 1997. Material for 4 weeks).

3. Kortright Davis *Emancipation Still Comin': Explorations in Caribbean Emancipatory Theology* (New York: Orbis Books, 1990), pp. 103–4.

4. Cain Hope Felder 'The Bible – Re-Contextualisation and the Black Religious Experience' in Gayraud S. Wilmore (ed.) *African American Religious Studies: An Interdisciplinary Anthology* (Durham and London: Duke University Press, 1989), p. 158.

5. Grant S. Shockley 'Black Theology and Religious Education' in Randolph Crump Miller (ed.) *Theologies of Religious Education* (Birmingham, Alabama: Religious Education Press, 1995), p. 333.

6. Cain Hope Felder (ed.) *Stony The Road We Trod: African American Biblical Interpretation* (Minneapolis: Augsburg Fortress, 1991).

7. Cain Hope Felder (ed.) *The African Heritage Study Bible* (Nashville, Tenn.: The James C. Winston Publishing Company, 1993).

8. See Volume 1 of *Growing into Hope: Believing and Expecting*, for opening section on *Heroes*, *Advent*, Week 3, p. 59.

9. Cain Hope Felder (ed.) *The African Heritage Study Bible* 'The Gospel of Matthew': Chapter 3, Verse 1, p. 1379.

10. Cain Hope Felder (ed.) *The African Heritage Study Bible*, pp.1827–32

11. Jeffrey N. Stinehelfer 'Dig This: The Revealing of Jesus Christ', *Religious Education* Vol. 64, No. 6, Nov.–Dec. 1969, p. 468.

12. Jeffrey N. Stinehelfer, 1969, p. 468.

13. P. K. Mc.Carey *The Black Bible Chronicles: From Genesis to the Promised Land [Book One]* (New York: African American Family Press, 1993); P. K.

Mc.Carey *The Black Bible Chronicles: Rappin' With Jesus [Book Two]* (New York: African American Family Press, 1994).

14. See Volume 2 of *Growing into Hope: Liberation and Change*, for section on *Pentecost*, Week 1, p. 128.

15. Earl Beckles 'The Language Needs of Children of West Indian Origin', *Multicultural Teaching* Vol. 8, No. 2, Spring 1990, pp. 38–41.

16. Carol Tomlin *Black Language Style in Sacred and Secular Texts* (New York: Caribbean Diaspora Press, 1999).

17. D. S. Massey and N. A. Denton *American Apartheid* (Cambridge, Massachusetts: Harvard, 1993), p. 164.

18. Grant S. Shockley 'Christian Education and the Black Religious Experience' in Charles R. Foster *Ethnicity in the Education of the Church* (Nashville, Tenn.: Conference papers/Scarritt Graduate School, Scarritt Press, 1987).

19. Grant S. Shockley, 1987, p.31.

20. Grant S. Shockley 'From Emancipation to Transformation to Consummation' in Marlene M. Mayr (ed.) *Does the Church Really Want Religious Education?* (Birmingham, Alabama: Religious Education Press, 1988), pp. 234–6.

21. See Volume 2 of *Growing into Hope: Liberation and Change*, for section on *Pentecost*, Week 2, pp. 137–56.

22. Ella P. Mitchell 'Oral Tradition: Legacy of Faith for the Black Church', *Religious Education* Vol. 81, No. 1, Winter 1986, pp. 100–1.

23. Joseph V. Crockett *Teaching Scripture from an African-American Perspective* (Nashville, Tenn.: Discipleship Resources, 1990).

24. See Volume 1 of *Growing into Hope: Believing and Expecting*, for section on *Advent*, Week 2 – 'Words and Stories', pp. 34–57

25. Joseph V. Crockett, 1990, pp. 15–26.

26. It should be noted that not all Black and Womanist theologians (in different locations of the world) feel that the theme of 'exile' is the dominant motif in Black theological reflection. Writers such as Lorraine Dixon prefer the theme of 'migration', viewing that as more representative of the African Caribbean experience. See Lorraine Dixon 'Are Vashti and Esther Our Sistas?' in Anthony G. Reddie (ed.) *Legacy: Anthology in Memory of Jillian Brown* (Peterborough: Methodist Publishing House, 1998), p. 97.

27. Henry H. Mitchell *Black Belief* (New York: Harper and Row, 1975), p. 49, Anthony G. Reddie *Faith, Stories and the Experience of Black Elders: Singing the Lord's Song in a Strange Land* (London: Jessica Kingsley Publishers, 2001), p. 43.

28. See Volume 2 of *Growing into Hope: Liberation and Change*, for the section on *Pentecost*, Week 2, pp. 137–56

29. The issue of intergenerational storytelling is addressed in greater detail in my previous book *Faith, Stories and the Experience of Black Elders* (2001).

30. Lawrence N. Jones 'Hope For Mankind: Insights From Black Religious History in the United States', *Journal of Religious Thought* Vol. 34, No. 2, Fall–Winter, 1978, p. 59.

31. Lawrence N. Jones, 1978, p. 59.

32. See Volume 1 of *Growing into Hope: Believing and Expecting*, for section on *Advent*, Week 1, pp. 14–32.

33. Lawrence N. Jones, 1978, p. 65.

34. Paulo Freire *Pedagogy of the Oppressed* (New York: Herder and Herder, 1970), p. 31.

35. Paulo Freire *Education for Critical Consciousness* (New York: Continuum, 1973), pp. 18–20.

36. Paulo Freire, 1970, p.33.

37. Paulo Freire, 1970, p. 53.

38. Paulo Freire, 1970, p. 58.

39. Paulo Freire, 1970, p. 58.

40. Paulo Freire, 1973.

41. Paulo Freire, 1973, pp. 3–58. See also his more recent *A Pedagogy of Hope: Relieving Pedagogy of the Oppressed* (New York: Continuum, 1999).

42. Paulo Freire and Ira Shor *A Pedagogy for Liberation: Dialogues for Transformative Education* (New York: MacMillan, 1987), pp. 8–9.

43. Freire and Shor, 1987, pp. 35–44.

44. James A. Banks (ed.) *Multicultural Education: Transformative Knowledge and Action* (New York: Teachers College Press, 1996), pp. 340–1.

45. James A. Banks, 1996, pp. 342–4.

46. See Volume 2 of *Growing into Hope: Liberation and Change*, for section on *Pentecost*, Week 2, pp. 154–5.

47. This is the author's preferred presentation of her name. An explanation for this is given in Robert Beckford *God of the Rhatid* (London: Darton, Longman, Todd, 2001), pp. 94–7.

48. bell hooks *Teaching to Transgress: Education as the Practice of Freedom* (New York: Routledge, 1994), pp. 93–128.

49. See Volume 1 of *Growing into Hope: Believing and Expecting*, particularly pp. 78, 83 and 88. See Volume 2 of *Growing into Hope: Liberation and Change*, particularly pp. 18, 20, 29, 56, 128, 142 and 154.

50. See Volume 1 of *Growing into Hope: Believing and Expecting*, particularly pp. 26–7, 52–5 and 100. See Volume 2 of *Growing into Hope: Liberation and Change*, particularly pp. 54, 59, 82–3, 104, 106–8, 128–9 and 139.

51. Anne Hope and Sally Timmel (illustrated by Chris Hodzi) *Training for Transformation: A Handbook for Community Workers*, in 4 volumes (Gweru, Zimbabwe: Mambo Press, 1999).

52. Paulo Freire, 1970, p. 31.

53. Hope and Timmel, 1999, p. 3.

54. Hope and Timmel, 1999, p. 8.

55. Paulo Freire, 1970, pp. 41–2.

56. Hope and Timmel, 1999, pp. 53–96.

57. Grant S. Shockley, 1987, p. 36.

58. Cheryl Bridges Johns *Pentecostal Formation: A Pedagogy among the*

Oppressed (Sheffield: Sheffield Academic Press, 1993), pp. 49–52.

59. Cheryl Bridges Johns, 1993, pp. 46–61.

60. Grant Shockley, 1987, p. 37.

61. See Volume 1 of *Growing into Hope: Believing and Expecting*, pp. 29–32.

62. James H. Cone 'Black Theology and the Black Church: Where Do We Go From Here?' in Gayraud S. Wilmore and James H. Cone (eds.) *Black Theology: A Documentary History, 1966–1979* (Maryknoll, New York: Orbis Books, 1979), pp. 350–9.

63. See Volume 1 of *Growing into Hope: Believing and Expecting*, pp. 29–32. Note the Bible passages that are highlighted from Matthew's Gospel and how these are linked to the exercise and the overall theme for that Sunday's lesson.

64. See Daniel S. Schipani 'Liberation Theology and Religious Education' in Randolph Crump Miller (ed.) *Theologies of Religious Education* (Birmingham, Alabama: Religious Education Press, 1995).

65. See Gustavo Gutierrez *A Theology of Liberation* (Maryknoll, New York: Orbis Books, 1973).

66. Daniel S. Schipani, 1995, pp. 288–9.

67. Daniel S. Schipani, 1995, p. 294.

68. See Volume 2 of *Growing into Hope: Liberation and Change*, pp.115–56.

69. Frank Marangos 'Liberation Theology and Christian Education Theory' in Jeff Astley, Leslie Francis and Colin Crowder (eds.) *Theological Perspectives on Christian Formation* (Grand Rapids, Michigan: W. B. Eerdmans, 1996), p. 192.

70. Frank Marangos, 1996, pp. 192–6.

71. Thomas Groome *Christian Religious Education* (San Francisco: Harper and Row, 1980), pp. 49–51.

72. Thomas Groome *Sharing Faith* (San Francisco: Harper, 1991).

73. Thomas Groome, 1991, p. 135.

74. Thomas Groome, 1991, pp. 138–51.

75. See Volume 2 of *Growing into Hope: Liberation and Change*, pp. 7–8.

76. Thomas Groome, 1991, pp. 151–3.

77. Thomas Groome, 1991, p. 153.

78. See Volume 2 of *Growing into Hope: Liberation and Change*, pp. 128–9.

79. Recent documentation has shown this to be a classic case of historic romanticism. In a report of the Joint Commission of the Three Methodist Churches on Sunday School Work to Conference 1931, it was noted that between them, the three traditions were writing off over '100,000 young people from their Sunday-School registers each year'. John Sutcliffe *Tuesday's Child: A Reader for Christian Education* (Birmingham: Christian Education Publishing, 2001), pp. 25–6.

80. For a useful description and analysis of the development of children's work within churches in Britain, see *The Child in the Church* (London: British Council of Churches, 1976), *Understanding Christian Nurture* (London: British Council of Churches, 1981), *Children in the Way* (London: The National Society and Church House Publishing, 1988), *All God's Children?* (London: The National Society and

Church House Publishing, 1991), *Unfinished Business* (London: CCBI Publications, 1995).

81. Winston James 'Migration, Racism and Identity Formation – The Caribbean Experience in Britain' in Winston James and Clive Harris (eds.) *Inside Babylon: The Caribbean Diaspora in Britain* (London: Verso, 1993), pp. 234–5.

82. See Anthony G. Reddie, 2001.

83. Thomas Groome, 1991, p. 156.

84. See *Growing into Hope: Believing and Expecting* and Volume 2 of *Growing into Hope: Liberation and Change* for the twelve thematic titles (six per volume), drawn from the discipline of Black theology. Accompanying these themes are short pieces of Black theological reflection.

85. See Volume 1 of *Growing into Hope: Believing and Expecting*, p. 10, for a brief summary of the process that gave rise to the materials in both volumes. Stages 3 and 4 represent the attempts by the author to engage with Christian religious education methods. Stages 2 and 5 represent attempts to engage with Black theological ideas, particularly in terms of developing thematic structure and an appropriate interpretative framework (or hermeneutic).

86. See Volume 1 of *Growing into Hope: Believing and Expecting*, p. 10.

87. See *Growing into Hope: Believing and Expecting*, p. 59.

88. *Growing into Hope: Believing and Expecting*, pp. 67–8.

89. *Growing into Hope: Believing and Expecting*, pp. 71–3.

90. Jerome Berryman G*odly Play: A Way of Religious Education* (New York: Harper Collins, 1991), pp. 1–3.

91. Clark C. Abt *Serious Games* (New York: Viking Press, 1970), p. 6.

92. Jerome Berryman, 1991, p. 7.

93. See Jean Piaget *Dreams and Imitation in Childhood* (New York: Norton, 1962) and *The Child and Reality* (New York: Penguin Books, 1976). Lawrence Kohlberg 'Stage and Sequence: The Cognitive Developmental Approach to Socialization' in David A. Goslin (ed.) *Handbook of Socialization Theory and Research* (Chicago: Rand McNally, 1969), pp. 347–480. See Erik Erikson *Childhood and Society* (New York: Norton, 1963) and *Identity, Youth and Crisis* (New York: Norton, 1968).

94. See Volume 2 of *Growing into Hope: Liberation and Change*, pp. 120–1.

95. 'Middle' equates approximately to Black children and young people aged between eight and eleven years of age.

96. 'Oldest' equates approximately to Black children and young people aged twelve and above.

97. 'Young' equates approximately to Black children aged between six and eight years of age.

98. K. Clark and M. Clark 'Identification and References in Negro Children' in E. Maccohy et al., (eds.) *Readings in Social Psychology* (New York: Holt, 1958).

99. Amos N. Wilson *Awakening the Natural Genius of Black Children* (New York: Afrikan World InfoSystems, 1991), p. 100.

100. See Volume 1 of *Growing into Hope: Believing and Expecting*, pp. 24–7.

101. See Volume 1 of *Growing into Hope: Believing and Expecting*, pp. 52–5. The words in question include: 'vex' (angry), 'pickney' (slang for child or children), 'frownsey' (dirty or grubby) and 'maugre' (exceptionally thin). The definitions in brackets are approximations. For further details see Emile L. Adams *Understanding Jamaican Patois* (Kingston, Jamaica: Kingston Publishers Ltd., 1991).

102. This term refers to the whole exercise of identifying aspects of the familial cultural experiences of these African-Caribbean children. These cultural experiences include issues of food, family and travel as depicted for example in the two stories in Volume 1 of *Growing into Hope: Believing and Expecting*, pp. 52–5.

103. Earl Beckles 'The Language Needs of Children of West Indian Origin', *Multicultural Teaching* Vol. 8, No. 2, Spring 1990, p. 39.

104. David Gillborn *'Race', Ethnicity and Education: Teaching and Learning in Multi-ethnic Schools* (London: Allen and Unwin, 1990), p. 182.

105. Walter Rodney *The Groundings with my Brothers* (New York: Grove Books, 1986), p. 33. See also Anthony G. Reddie, 2001, pp. 101–10.

106. Robert Beckford has identified the important relationship and interplay between Black religiosity and Black popular cultural expression. He has analysed the ways in which Black people often use trickery and subterfuge to survive and thrive in often hostile environments. Language is an important tool in this survival ethic. See *Jesus Is Dread* (London: Darton, Longman and Todd, 1998) and *Dread and Pentecostal* (London: SPCK, 2000).

107. The development of Patois in particular and Creole in general owes much to the syncretism between traditional languages spoken by African slaves transported from that continent to the Caribbean, and the English language, spoken by their slave masters. The development and existence of these linguistic forms was suppressed and stigmatized by the White plantocracy as a means of asserting their control over the ontological selfhood and identity of the African slave. Yet these idioms persisted, partly as a form of resistance, and in part, as a means of connoting identity and selfhood. In more recent times, there has been a considerable debate in Caribbean societies and within the many churches in the Caribbean relating to the efficacy of these idioms. In the context of church life, contemporary Caribbean Christian educators have argued that the appropriation of such linguistic forms can play an important role within the liturgical and educational life of the church. Through their status as being indicative of the indigenous expression of identity and self-worth, this facet of everyday life can provide the foundational components for the development of a contextualized theology that will ultimately assist in the liberation of the Caribbean church. For further information see Joyce Bailey *'Fashion Me A People*: A New Ecumenical Caribbean Curriculum', *Religious Education* Vol. 75, No. 5, Sept.–Oct. 1980, pp. 577–91, Michael Clarke *Reclaiming the Black Experience in the Anglican Church in Barbados: A Study Amongst a Group of Young Anglicans* (Unpublished D. Min. thesis, Toronto School of Theology, Trinity College, Ontario, 1995), pp. 45–55, Robert W. M. Cuthbert *Ecumenism and Development: A Socio-historical Analysis of the Caribbean Conference of Churches* (Bridgetown, Barbados: Caribbean Conference of Churches, 1986). For an analy-

sis of Jamaican Patois, see Emile L. Adams *Understanding Jamaican Patois* (Kingston, Jamaica: Kingston Publishers Ltd, 1991) and Carol Tomlin *Black Language Style in Sacred and Secular Contexts* (Brooklyn, New York: Caribbean Diaspora Press, 1999).

108. Janice Hale-Benson *Black Children: Their Roots, Culture and Learning Styles* (Baltimore: The Johns Hopkins University Press, 1986), p. 68.

109. See British Council of Churches/Council of Churches of Britain and Ireland reports, *Bible and Children* 1988, *Children in the Church* 1976, *Children and Holy Communion* 1989, *Understanding Christian Nurture* 1981 and *Unfinished Business* 1995. See note 80 (in this chapter) for publishing details.

110. See Volume 2 of *Growing into Hope: Liberation and Change*, p. 133.

111. See Volume 2 of *Growing into Hope: Liberation and Change*, pp. 142–3.

112. Janice Hale-Benson, 1986, pp. 84–6.

113. Michael Ross *Building Positive Images in African American Males Through the Sunday School, from a Black Perspective* (Unpublished D. Min. thesis, Chicago: United Theological Seminar, 1993), p. 157.

114. *Kwesi* – Knowledge, Education and Support. In the early 1990s, *Kwesi* was formed. It was a mentoring scheme originated by Gilroy Brown and Guy Woolery, that sought to work with African Caribbean males in state schools in Birmingham, particularly those at risk from exclusion. For further details see Reva Klein 'Escape Route from the Fire of Alienation', *Times Educational Supplement* No. 4102, 10 February 1995, Section 2, p. 6, and Henrietta Bond 'Absent without Leave', *Community Care* No. 1135, 29 August 1996, pp. 22–3.

115. Christine Challender *Education For Empowerment: The Practice and Philosophies of Black Teachers* (Stoke-on-Trent: Trentham Books, 1997), pp. 97–132 and 156–66.

116. Tony Sewell *Black Masculinities and Schooling* (Stoke-on-Trent: Trentham Books, 1997), pp. 25–66.

117. Cecile Wright, Debbie Weekes and Alex McGlaughan (eds.) *'Race', Class and Gender in Exclusion from School* (London: Falmer Press, 2000), pp. 54–62.

118. Diana T. Slaughter 'The Education of Black Youth as a Cultural Problem', *Criterion* Vol. 14, Autumn 1975, p. 11.

119. Urie Bronfenbrenner 'Ecological Systems Theory' in Ross Vasta (ed.) *Six Theories of Child Development* (London: Jessica Kingley, 1992), p. 190.

120. Urie Bronfenbrenner, 1992, p. 190.

121. Janice Hale-Benson, 1986, p. 103.

122. See Volume 2 of *Growing into Hope: Liberation and Change*, pp. 8–10.

123. Janice Hale-Benson, 1986, p. 8.

Chapter 4: Making it Work

1. See the previous chapter for the discussion on how the *Advent* and *Pentecost* sections of *Growing into Hope* were created.

2. Kortright Davis *Emancipation Still Comin': Explorations in Caribbean Emancipatory Theology* (New York: Orbis Books, 1990), p. 70.

3. Kortright Davis, 1990, p. 80–5.

4. Michael Clarke *Reclaiming the Black Experience in the Anglican Church of Barbados: A Study Amongst a Group of Young Anglicans* (Unpublished D. Min. thesis, Toronto School of Theology, Trinity College, Ontario, 1995), pp. 100–11.

5. This principle should be taken with some caution, as I am anxious that we should not romanticize the endemic poverty of the Caribbean. The special place accorded them in God's creation should not be seen as adequate recompense for the ills of globalization, neo-colonialism and post-imperialism

6. A. Shorter *Towards a Theology of Inculturation* (New York: Orbis Books, 1988), pp. 59–85.

7. A. Wade Boykin 'Psychological/Behavioural Verve in Academic/Task Performance: Pre-Theoretical Considerations', *Journal of Negro Education* No. 47, 1978, pp. 343–54.

8. A. Wade Boykin, 1978, pp. 346–54.

9. A. Wade Boykin, 1978, p. 346.

10. A. Wade Boykin, 1978, p. 347.

11. Tony Sewell *Black Masculinities and Schooling* (Stoke-on-Trent: Trentham Books, 1997), pp. 196–9.

12. See Volume 1 of *Growing into Hope: Believing and Expecting*, pp.136–7 and the story, 'Time Fi Go a Market'.

13. In Methodist terms this denotes a trained and authorized preacher and leader of worship who is not ordained. Other traditions may term these individuals 'lay readers' or 'lay pastors'.

14. See Volume 1 of *Growing into Hope: Believing and Expecting*, pp.136–7.

15. See Volume 1 of *Growing into Hope: Believing and Expecting*, Appendices 14, 15 and 16.

16. This theme is explored in greater depth in my previous book *Faith, Stories and the Experience of Black Elders: Singing the Lord's Song in a Strange Land* (London: Jessica Kingsley, 2001).

17. Ella P. Mitchell 'Oral Tradition: The Legacy of Faith for the Black Church', *Religious Education* Vol. 81, No. 1, Winter 1986, pp. 93–112.

18. Charles R. Foster *Teaching in the Community of Faith* (Nashville, Tenn.: Abingdon Press, 1982), p. 54. See also *Educating Congregations: The Future of Christian Education* (Nashville, Tenn.: Abingdon Press, 1994).

19. See Volume 1 of *Growing into Hope: Believing and Expecting* and Volume 2 of *Growing into Hope: Liberation and Change*, for the various plays and interactive stories contained in the text.

20. See Volume 1 of *Growing into Hope: Believing and Expecting*, p. 130.

21. See Volume 1 of *Growing into Hope: Believing and Expecting*, p. 135 for this exercise.

22. See Volume 1 of *Growing into Hope: Believing and Expecting*, pp. 136–7. Evadne and Jelani's father read this story as part of the all-age harvest festival

service at this Methodist church. The children were encouraged to participate as the story was being read.

23. See John H. Westerhoff III *Will Our Children Have Faith?* (New York: Seabury Press, 1976), *Living the Faith Community* (San Francisco: Harper and Row, 1985), 'The Liturgical Imperative of Religious Education' in James Michael Lee (ed.) *The Religious Education We Need* (Birmingham, Alabama: Religious Education Press, 1977).

24. C. D. Coleman 'Agenda for the Black Church', *Religious Education* Vol. 64, No. 6, Nov.–Dec. 1969. Bonita Pope Curry 'The Role of the Church in the Educational Development of Black Children' in Lee N. June (ed.) *The Black Family* (Grand Rapids, Michigan: Zondervan Publishing, 1991). James D. Tyms 'The Black Church as an Ally in the Education of Black Children', *Journal Of Religious Thought* Vol. 36, No. 2, 1979–80.

25. Charles R. Foster 'The Pastor: Agent of Vision in the Education of a Community of Faith' in Robert L. Browning (ed.) *The Pastor as Religious Educator* (Birmingham, Alabama: Religious Education Press, 1987), p. 22.

26. Charles R. Foster, 1987, p. 25.

27. Charles R. Foster 'Abundance of Managers – Scarcity of Teachers', *Religious Education* Vol. 80, No. 3, Summer 1985, pp. 437–46.

28. Charles R. Foster, 1985, p. 446.

29. Allen J. Moore 'An Educational Approach to Renewing Local Churches', *Religious Education* Vol. 64, No. 6, Nov.–Dec. 1969, pp. 472–9.

30. See Edward P. Wimberly *Pastoral Care in the Black Church* (Nashville, Tenn.: Abingdon, 1979), *African American Pastoral Care* (Nashville, Tenn.: Abingdon, 1991), *Moving from Shame to Self-Worth* (Nashville, Tenn.: Abingdon, 1999). Emmanuel Y. Lartey *In Living Colour* (London: Cassell, 1997).

31. Anthony G. Reddie *Faith, Stories and the Experience of Black Elders: Singing the Lord's Song in a Strange Land* (London: Jessica Kingsley, 2001).

32. Anthony G. Reddie, 2001, pp. 47–61.

33. Anthony G. Reddie, 2001, pp. 107–10.

34. Hilary Beckles *Black Rebellion in Barbados: The Struggle against Slavery, 1627–1838* (Bridgetown, Barbados: Carib Research and Publications Inc. 1987), p. 52. See also S. Hall 'Religious Ideologies and Social Movements in Jamica' in R. Bocock and K. Thompson (eds.) *Religion and Ideology* (Manchester: Manchester University Press, 1985).

35. Grant S. Shockley 'Christian Education and the Black Religious Experience' in Charles R. Foster (ed.) *Ethnicity in the Education of the Church* (Nashville, Tenn.: Conference Papers/Scarritt Graduate School, Scarritt Press, 1987), p. 38.

36. Grant S. Shockley, 1987, p. 39.

37. See Carter G. Woodson *The Mis-Education of the Negro* (New Jersey: Trenton World Press, [1933], 1990). See also Robert Beckford *Jesus Is Dread* (London: Darton, Longman, Todd, 1998), pp. 43–58.

38. Matthew 18.15–20.

39. Thomas E. Leyland *Developing a Model of Religious Education for Black*

Southern Baptist Churches (Unpublished Ed. D. dissertation, Southern Baptist Theological Seminary, 1982), p. 123.

40. Letty Russell 'Christian Religious Education and the Inner City' in Donald B. Rogers (ed.) *Urban Church Education* (Birmingham, Alabama: Religious Education Press, 1989), p. 33.

41. Letty Russell, 1989, p. 33.

42. See Chapter 1, where this issue is addressed in socio-political and cultural terms.

43. A number of years ago there was an exhibition at the public art gallery in Birmingham of images of Jesus throughout the centuries. In more recent times, post-colonial theologians have sought to locate Jesus within the cultural and social world that spoke to their experiences as people of colour. In these later images, Jesus was Asian, dressed in clothes and pictured in scenes that identified him with South and South-East Asia. In the visitors' book situated at the end of the exhibition, a number of people commented that it was blasphemy to portray Jesus as Asian – he was, after all, Jewish. Yet, in the earlier pictures of Jesus in the exhibition, dating from the Renaissance, the figure of Christ was no more Jewish than in the later pictures. The difference between the two was that in the earlier pictures, he was White. The objection to the post-colonial pictures, therefore, was not Jesus' lack of Jewish identity, it was the fact that he was not White.

44. In effect, what I am saying is, if we stripped candidating procedures of any metaphysical spiritualized reality (i.e., the Holy Spirit does not mediate God's presence upon the process), and made it a self-consciously human decision-making construct, what would the end-product be? Who would be accepted to train for ordained ministry? My answer is that nothing would be changed. The same people (overwhelmingly White, middle-class and professional) would be chosen. The notion that it is God who is in the business of choosing people and not solely human beings who exercise ecclesial power is one I would like to challenge.

45. See Acts 2.36, 1 Cor. 12.3, 1 Cor. 16.22, Philippians 2.5–11 for references to the lordship of Christ.

46. See William R. Herzog II *Jesus, Justice and the Reign of God: A Ministry of Liberation* (Louisville, Kentucky: John Knox Press, 2000).

47. See Robert Beckford, 1998, and William David Spencer *Dread Jesus* (London: SPCK, 1999).

48. See the 'Black liberationist Bible study' in Chapter 2.

49. See Thomas Groome *Christian Religious Education* (San Francisco: Harper and Row, 1980), Chapter 7, and Daniel Schipani *Religious Education Encounters Liberation Theology* (Birmingham, Alabama: Religious Education Press, 1988), Chapter 3.

50. Black children are identified as being the most marginalized within the church, on the grounds of age, the negation of Black culture and experiences, and their relative powerlessness. Children are the least able to effect changes in the church. Often, their very presence within the church is wholly dependent upon significant others. In the majority of cases, children require an adult to take them

to and from church. Given the complexities of family life since the late 1960s, relating, particularly, to fragmented families due in part to the number of divorces, children are often expected to visit a parent that is living in separate circumstances from the child or the rest of family. The expectations of having to visit a separated parent over the course of a weekend may prevent a child from being able to attend church. The marginalization of children is compounded by the lack of awareness of the psychological effects that may arise through the prevailing culture of dependency that is evident in the lives of children and the reality of being brought to church whether the child wants to attend church or not. The lack of awareness of the importance of Black popular, expressive cultures in the lives of Black children and its absence within the worship and celebratory life of the church only adds to their sense of estrangement and disaffection.

51. Herbert Posch Altrichter, Peter and Bridget Somekh *Teachers Investigating their Work* (London: Routledge, 1993), p. 102.

52. See the previous chapter for the outline and brief analysis of this service.

Chapter 5: The Way it Should Be?

1. The material for *Lent* and *Easter* was written as four weeks of teaching and learning material, comprising Mothering Sunday, Passion Sunday, Palm Sunday and Easter Sunday. The material was written in December 1996 and completed in January 1997. It was piloted in inner-city churches in Birmingham in March 1997.

2. See Volume 2 of *Growing into Hope: Liberation and Change*, pp. 12 and 92.

3. James H. Cone *A Black Theology of Liberation* (New York: Orbis, 1986), p. 85.

4. James H. Cone, 1986, pp. 85–6.

5. James H. Cone, 1986, pp. 87–103.

6. James H. Cone *God of the Oppressed* (San Francisco: Harper San Francisco, 1975), p. 138.

7. James H. Cone, 1975, p. 138.

8. Dwight N. Hopkins *(Introducing) Black Theology of Liberation* (Maryknoll, New York: Orbis, 1999), pp. 41–8.

9. See Volume 2 of *Growing into Hope: Liberation and Change*. Refer to pictures at the rear of this volume, Appendix 11–17.

10. See *Growing into Hope: Liberation and Change*, Appendix 12.

11. See Volume 2 of *Growing into Hope: Liberation and Change*, pp. 7–8, for an exercise entitled 'Are We in the Story?' This exercise was an attempt to assist Black youth and the individuals who teach them to look at the Bible and to see themselves represented within the narratives of Scripture.

12. See Carter G. Woodson *The Miseducation of the Negro* (First published 1933. Republished Trenton, New Jersey: Africa World Press, 1990). See also Walter Rodney *The Groundings with my Brothers* (New York: Grove Books, 1986), pp. 16–34.

13. Na'im Akbar *Chains and Images of Psychological Slavery* (Jersey City: New Mind Publications, 1978). Edward Coard *How The West Indian Child is Made Educationally Subnormal in the British School System: The Scandal of the Black Child in Britain* (London: New Beacon Books, 1971). Jawanza Kunjufu *Countering the Conspiracy to Destroy Black Boys*, 3 volumes (Chicago: African American Images, 1982–1990). Useni Eugene Perkins *Harvesting New Generations: The Positive Development of Black Youth* (Chicago: Third World Press, 1986).

14. Emmanuel Chukwudi Eze *Race and the Enlightenment* (Massachusetts: Blackwell, 1997), pp. 29–94.

15. A process whereby an individual is denied the opportunity to conceive of themselves or to be treated as a subjective individual, where the meaning surrounding one's existence is defined by the subject themselves. Rather, the individual is denied any subjective status, and is reduced to an object. Meaning and definition for the individual is imposed from without (by an external body or bodies, usually with power and by coercive means), rather than from within. In effect, the individual becomes an object. Objects are named by those who possess the power, and can deploy the necessary language to 'name' the reality of the 'other'.

16. Stuart Hall 'Cultural Identity and Diaspora' in bell hooks (ed.) *Black Looks: Race and Representation* (London: Turnaround Press, 1992), p. 3.

17. Jawanza Kunjufu *Developing Positive Self-Images and Discipline in Black Children* (Chicago: African American Images, 1984), pp. 27–8.

18. Romney Moseley *Becoming A Self Before God: Critical Transformations* (Nashville, Tenn.: Abingdon Press, 1991), pp. 102–4.

19. Craig Ellison (ed.) *Your Better Self* (San Francisco: Harper and Row, 1983), p. 11.

20. See Volume 2 of *Growing into Hope: Liberation and Change*, pp. 94–113.

21. See Volume 2 of *Growing into Hope: Liberation and Change*, Appendix 9.

22. See Volume 2 of *Growing into Hope: Liberation and Change*, pp. 79–81.

23. Most usually identified as an adult-orientated concern given expression in adult-dominated worship.

24. The perception of Christian learning is often seen as a child-orientated activity given expression in Sunday school/junior church.

25. See *Children in the Way: New Directions for the Church's Children*. A report from the General Synod Board of Education. (London: National Society/Church House Publishing, 1993), pp. 55–60.

26. See Debra Dean Murphy 'Worship as Catechesis: Knowledge, Desire and Christian Formation', *Theology Today* October 2001, pp. 321–32. Murphy gives an excellent argument for the need to hold worship and learning together. The effective development of the latter is achieved through the words, actions and symbols of the former.

27. Jeff Astley 'Growing into Christ: The Psychology and Politics of Christian Maturity' in Jeff Astley and David Day (eds.) *The Contours of Christian Education* (Great Wakering, Essex: McCrimmon, 1992), p. 317.

28. Avery Dulles *Models of the Church* (New York: Doubleday, 1987), pp. 204–26.

29. *Unfinished Business: Children and the Churches*. The Consultative Group on Ministry among Children. (London: CCBI Publications, 1995), pp. 21–3.

30. Michael Clarke *Reclaiming the Black Experience in the Anglican Church in Barbados: A Study Amongst a Group of Young Anglicans* (Unpublished D. Min. thesis, Toronto School of Theology, Trinity College, Ontario, 1995), p. 118.

31. Romney Moseley 'Retrieving Intergenerational and Intercultural Faith' in Charles R. Foster and Grant S. Shockley (eds.) *Working with Black Youth* (Nashville, Tenn.: Abingdon Press, 1989), pp. 77–99.

32. Anthony G. Reddie 'A Theology of Good Intentions' in Stuart J. Burgess *Coming of Age: Challenges and Opportunities in the 21st Century* (York: Stuart J. Burgess, 1999), pp. 89–94.

33. See Harold A. Carter *The Prayer Tradition of Black People* (Baltimore, Gateway Press, 1984), pp. 80–109.

34. The term 'myth' in this context accords with the views of Ivan Strensky in *Four Theories of Myth in the Twentieth Century* (Iowa City: The University of Iowa Press, 1986), p. 37. Strensky asserts that from a biblical and theological perspective, a myth is defined as being the means of communication between a transcendent God and the contingency of humankind. Human beings cannot talk of God, relying solely upon rational language, but make recourse to mythical language that is concerned with the divine–human encounter. Myths in this sense should not be seen as denoting a naturalistic form of facticity, as one might approach the natural sciences. Neither does it imply, however, that mythical narratives are simply meaningless statements.

35. Jacquelyn Grant, 'A Theological Framework' in Charles R. Foster and Grant S. Shockley (eds.) *Working with Black Youth: Opportunities for Christian Ministry* (Nashville, Tenn.: Abingdon Press, 1989), p. 66.

36. James H. Cone, 1986, pp. 69–70.

37. James H. Cone, 1986, pp. 70–3.

38. Robert Beckford *God of the Rahtid* (London: Darton, Longman and Todd, pp. 98–112.

39. Olivia Pearl Stokes 'Black Theology: A Challenge to Religious Education' in Norma H. Thompson (ed.) *Religious Education and Theology* (Birmingham, Alabama: Religious Education Press, 1982), pp. 97–8.

40. Craig Ellison, 1983, p. 11.

41. See Emmanuel Y. Lartey *In Living Colour: An Intercultural Approach to Pastoral Care and Counselling* (London: Cassell, 1997), pp. 85–107.

42. Useni Eugene Perkins *Harvesting New Generations: The Positive Development of Black Youth* (Chicago: Third World Press, 1986), pp. 79–115.

43. See Winston James 'Migration, Racism and Identity' in Winston James and Clive Harris (eds.) *Inside Babylon* (London: Verso, 1993). Also Ron Ramdin *Reimaging Britain: 500 Hundred Years of Black and Asian History* (London: Pluto Press, 1999), pp. 141–90 and 258–305.

44. This refers to an informal collective savings scheme in which a number of people each agree to put a set amount of money into a collective pot on a weekly, bi-weekly or monthly basis. The set amount, which is agreed in advance, is called a 'hand'. On a rotation basis, the sum of the deposited money is given to one individual. This system allowed many early African-Caribbean migrants to raise the necessary funds to put deposits on houses or to send for immediate relatives from the Caribbean to join them in Britain.

45. See William David Spencer *Dread Jesus* (London: SPCK, 1999).

46. Joseph V. Crockett *Teaching Scripture: From an African-American Perspective* (Nashville, Tenn.: Discipleship Resources, 1989), pp. 39–52.

47. See Michael Ross *Building Positive Images in African American Males Through the Sunday School from a Black Perspective* (Unpublished D. Min. thesis, United Theological Seminary, 1993).

48. See Jeremiah A. Wright Jnr 'Unashamedly Black and Unapologetically Christian' in Michael I. N. Dash, L. Rita Dixon, Darius L. Swann and Ndugu T'Ofori-Atta (eds.) *African Roots: Towards an Afrocentric Christian Witness* (Lithonia, Georgia: SCP/Third World Literature, 1994), pp. 178–95.

49. Mike Vance 'Changing Expectations: Working with Disaffected African Caribbean Boys', *Multicultural Teaching* Vol. 15, No. 2, Spring 1997, pp. 30–43.

50. Corinne Julius 'Trainers Score in Extra Time', *Times Educational Supplement* 4263, 13 March 1998, pp. 16–17.

51. George S. Richards 'Supplementary Schools – Their Service to Education', *Multicultural Teaching* Vol. 14, No. 1, Autumn 1995, p. 6.

52. See Chapter 2 for a description of and the role played by supplementary schools in Black communities in Britain.

53. Romney Moseley, 1991, p. 89.

54. Romney Moseley, 1991, pp. 90–100.

55. Romney Moseley , 1991, p. 92.

56. Anne S. Wimberly *Soul Stories: African American Christian Education* (Nashville, Tenn.: Abingdon Press, 1994).

57. Evelyn L. Parker *Twenty Seeds of Hope: Religious Moral Values in African American Adolescents in Chicago and Implications for Christian Education in the Black Church* (Unpublished Ph. D. thesis, Garret/Northwestern Program in Religious and Theological Studies, 1996), pp. 46–147.

58. Anthony G. Reddie *Faith, Stories and the Experience of Black Elders: Singing the Lord's Song in a Strange Land* (London: Jessica Kingsley, 2001). See the schema for intergenerational conversations entitled 'Sharing Experiences Between People of Different Generations: The Oral Tradition Document'.

59. Anthony G. Reddie, 2001. See 'The Impact of the Oral Tradition Conversations on Black Children', pp. 77–99.

60. This phrase refers to the physical act of delivering your 'hand' or share of the collective pot to the person responsible for overseeing the pardner. Often the 'hand' is thrown (theatrically in some cases) onto the table where the money is being assembled – hence the use of the term 'throw'.

61. Anthony G. Reddie, 2001. See the introductory sketch entitled 'Looking Ahead', for an example of Black elders reflecting on their experience of 'exile' in Britain in the late 1950s and early 1960s.

62. Edith D. Thomas, Anne S. Wimberly and Edward P. Wimberly 'Honoring and Sharing Our Elders' Wisdom' in Anne S. Wimberly (ed.) *Honoring African American Elders* (San Francisco: Josey-Bass, 1997), pp. 171–85.

63. Michael I. N. Dash, Jonathan Jackson, Stephen C. Rasor *Hidden Wholeness* (Cleveland, Ohio: United Church Press, 1997).

64. Dash, Jackson, Rasor, 1997, pp. 76–103.

65. Dash, Jackson, Rasor, 1997, pp. 104–32.

66. At the consultation for Black youth (reference to which has been made previously in this chapter), the participants were asked to list the things they would like to see in the church, alongside those aspects of the church that were not so pleasant. Prevalent, on both the positive and the negative lists, was the issue of music in the church. The present musical policy in the majority of inner-city historic-mainline churches in the project was the traditional European hymnody dating from the eighteenth and nineteenth centuries. The majority of these young people wanted Black popular forms of music, indicative and reflective of Black experience and culture – music that was rhythmical and dynamic. For further details, see James H. Cone *The Spirituals and the Blues* (New York: Seabury Press, 1972), Eugene Genovese *Roll, Jordan Roll: The World the Slaves Made* (New York: Pantheon, 1974), Michael W. Harris *The Rise of the Gospel Blues: The Music of Thomas Andrew Dorsey in the Urban Church* (New York: Oxford University Press, 1992), Arthur C. Jones *Wade in the Water: The Wisdom of the Spirituals* (Maryknoll, New York: Orbis, 1993).

67. Nelson Copeland *The Heroic Revolution: A New Agenda for Urban Youth Work* (Nashville, Ten.: James C. Winston Publishing Company, 1995), pp. 15–21.

68. William R. Myers 'Models for Urban Youth Ministry: Goals, Styles and Contexts' in Donald B. Rogers (ed.) *Urban Church Education* (Birmingham, Alabama: Religious Education Press, 1989), p. 130.

69. James H. Cone, 1972, pp. 9–127.

70. Robert Beckford *Jesus is Dread* (London: Darton, Longman and Todd, 1998), pp. 130–44.

71. This phrase was a commonplace metaphor for describing the notion of being/feeling comfortable and at ease within any social setting. Many of the young people felt that church was not a context where they could be their authentic selves. See also the exercise 'Dancing at Home and Dancing Abroad', in Volume 2 of *Growing into Hope: Liberation and Change*, pp. 8–10.

72. The group consists of Joanne Smith, Carol Troupe and Sam Wilkinson (principal songwriter and arranger). Their first album, entitled *Soul Spirit*, was released in July 2000 by Fortune and Glory, an independent company in Moseley, Birmingham.

73. Peter Brierley (ed.) *UK Christian Handbook – Religious Trends 2000/2001* No. 2 (London: Christian Research/Harpercollins, 1999).

Index